THE BEST

HIKES & WALKS
ON & AROUND
MT HOOD

Sonia Buist

with

Emily Keller & Sandy Mooney

LOLITS PRESS
Portland, Oregon

Previously published as *Hikes & Walks on Mt Hood* and *Around & About Mount Hood,* 2nd editions by Sonia Buist & Emily Keller, LOLITS Press, © 2007 & 2013.

ISBN: 978-0-9643836-3-0

Writer: Sonia Buist

Illustrations & Maps: Emily Keller & Sandy Mooney

Cover photo: Trillium Lake and Mt Hood

Formatting & layout: Paul Erdman, Creative Progression

LOLITS is an acronym for **Little Old Ladies in Tennis Shoes.**
Copies of *The BEST Hikes & Walks on & Around Mt Hood* can be ordered from:
- LOLITS Press website: www.mthoodhiking.com
- Email: mthoodhiking@aol.com
- By phone: 503 292 0237
- And in many Northwest outdoor & bookstores, local stores & Museum & Information Center in Gov't Camp, US Forest Service Offices, Amazon.com and Timberline Lodge

By the same author, *Hikes & Walks on Mt Hood* and *Around & About Mt Hood : Exploring the Timberline Trail, Access Trails & Day Hikes* also available from LOLITS Press

TABLE OF CONTENTS

Long Hikes

Map of the Timberline Trail

Long Hikes accessing the Timberline
Trail on north side of Mt Hood

How the Forest Recovers from a Fire

Useful Information

Mount Hood's Glaciers are Melting

Index

Acknowledgements

We would like to acknowledge the help and support we got for this project from many of our friends. Special thanks to Dale Rush, Susan & Bill Sack, Anne Ashford and Linda Bedard for their invaluable help in re-hiking all of the trails in this book and the laborious task of editing. We would also like to acknowledge the important contributions of all who helped with *Hikes & Walks* and *Around & About Mount Hood* and Debbie Asakawa, who provided many of the photos.

Permission was kindly given by the Oregon Historical Society for the reproduction of the photograph on page 58 of the Summit of Mt Hood, 1896 (Zenus Moody Family, #OrHi 37884), by The Oregonian for the graphic on page 118 of the glaciers on Mt Hood, and by Keith Jackson for the graphic on page 119 of the glacier melt on Mt Hood. The section on River Crossing Safety Guidelines is excerpted from signs donated by friends and family of Sarah Bishop, a skilled hiker and lover of wilderness, who died tragically on the Sandy River in 2004 when the river was unseasonably high, with permission from the Bishop family.

Thanks also to other hikers who helped with checking the hikes:

Steve Kemper
Leah Cronn
Justin Denny
Joan Wellsmore

Karen Casey-Tatom
Gregg Smith
Jannell Werner

Mt Hood from Bald Mountain

Elk Cove

Introduction & How to Use this Book

Oregon has a well-deserved reputation for its natural beauty. It is less well known for its hiking trails although few countries, much less states, match Oregon for its range and variety of hiking. We are particularly fortunate in having two spectacular areas for hiking within 60 miles of Portland—the Columbia Gorge and the Mt Hood areas.

This book focuses on the Government Camp and Timberline Lodge areas on Mt Hood, both close enough to Portland for half-day or day hikes. Hiking on Mt Hood offers magnificent mountain scenery, beautiful forests— some with majestic old-growth trees—streams, rivers, wetlands, abundant flowers, huckleberries, birds and glimpses of wildlife. Some of the hikes include segments of the Timberline Trail, the 41-mile necklace around Mt Hood that drops in and climbs out of canyons carved by the rivers that flow from the many glaciers on the mountain.

This book follows the two other LOLITS Press guides to Mt Hood: *Hikes & Walks on Mt Hood* and *Around & About Mt Hood: Exploring the Timberline Trail, Access Trails and Day Hikes*, and includes a selection of what we consider to be the "best", grouping them by length: short, medium-length and long. We have also added some new trails and information about cross-country and snowshoe trails to make this an all-season guide.

We hope that this book will serve to introduce you to new walking and hiking trails and areas. We have tried to include hikes that cover a range of difficulty and chal- lenge, from a short walk suitable for those with limited mobility, to trails with appreciable elevation gain and difficult terrain. We encourage you to try some new hikes and venture away from the heavily-used trails.

Mt Hood is also a spectacular winter playground with several downhill ski areas and many areas that offer outstanding cross-country skiing and snowshoeing. This book includes information about trails for cross-country skiing and snowshoeing in and around Government Camp—see table on page 15 "Cross-Country/Snowshoe Trails" and map on page 16 "Map of Cross-Country/Snowshoe Trails." A snowflake icon ❋ in the description of hikes in this book identifies a trail that is designated as a Cross-Country/Snowshoe Trail by the Forest Service. Trails also have blue diamond markers on the trees.

Mt Hood in Winter from Summit Ski Area

We wanted to make this a book that tucks comfortably into a pocket. This imposed constraints on the amount of text we could include and on the size of maps. Our overriding aim was to be precise and accurate. We hope we have struck a balance that works for most people.

HELPFUL WEBSITES

There are a number of excellent websites that provide invaluable up-to-date information. We suggest you use them to check current conditions and accessibility for your planned outdoor adventures.

Mt Hood Information Center   *www.mthood.info*

This is a very well-organized site that is crammed with information including weather and road conditions; guides to lodging, dining, shopping and forest recreation; news and events; links to the Forest Service Trail information and to Virtual Hikes by NW Hiker.

US Forest Service   *www.fs.fed.us/r6/mthood*

Another superb site offering masses of information, arranged in a user-friendly format that includes passes and permits, detailed description of trails, current weather and trail conditions and campgrounds.

Mt Hood's Alpine Village:
http://www.mounthoodinfo.com

ACCESS & PERMITS

A *North*west *Forest Pass* (annual, day or online ePass) is required at many trailheads in Oregon and may be purchased at Forest District offices and other local businesses & stores.

A *Senior Pass* for 62 years and older is honored nationwide at most Forest Service sites and campgrounds including National Park Service, BLM, and US Fish & Wildlife Service sites charging entrance or standard amenity fees.

A *Wilderness Permit* is required for hiking in the Mt Hood Wilderness and is obtained (free) by signing in at the Wilderness Permit Boxes on the access trails. Be sure to stop, sign in and carry a copy of the permit. Present regulations limit groups (including dogs and horses) to 12.

A *Sno-Park Permit* (day or annual) is required for parking in Sno-Parks in winter. Information about the location of Sno-Parks is available at *www.fs.fed. us/r6/mthood*.

HOW HIKES ARE CATEGORIZED

We have grouped the hikes into *Short, Medium-Length, and Long*. The long hikes are also divided into those that access the Timberline Trail on the north side of Mt Hood and those that don't. We have tried to provide guidance as to the relative difficulty of the trails and the noteworthy features of each hike. To rank the trails by difficulty, we have taken into account the length, elevation gain, smoothness of the trail, the altitude of the segment and other features such as river crossings. The categories we have used are *Easy, Moderately Strenuous, Strenuous,* and *Very Strenuous.* We have given estimated duration for the hikes but these times should be thought of as very rough estimates recognizing that people vary in their hiking pace and in the time they spend enjoying the scenery, identifying the flowers, taking photographs, and just lingering. Cross-Country/Snowshoe trails are ranked by the Forest Service as *Easy, More Difficult* and *Most Difficult*.

HIKING WITH KIDS OR FOR THOSE WITH LIMITED MOBLILITY

The *Table of Hikes* on pages 12-14 includes a suggestion about which hikes work well for kids and for those with limited mobility. The distance and time for each hike will also help to guide you.

CAR SECURITY

Unfortunately, theft from cars has become a problem at many trailheads. It is not a good idea to leave anything valuable in the car.

HIKING SAFETY

IT IS NOT A GOOD IDEA TO HIKE ALONE. If you do, you might want to consider taking a cell phone but be warned that there are many areas in the mountains with no coverage and be sure to tell someone where you

are going. The cell phone should only be used to call for help *if there is a serious emergency.* A call requires the County Sheriff to initiate a response from the appropriate responders. To use it otherwise is to waste the precious resources of the Forest Service and other groups involved in mountain rescues.

However short you expect a hike to be, it's always a good idea to be prepared for the unexpected. Many groups offer a list of useful items. For example, the *list of 10 essentials recommended by REI includes:*

1. Navigation (map and compass)
2. Sun protection (sunglasses and sunscreen)
3. Insulation (extra clothing)
4. Illumination (headlamp/flashlight)
5. First-aid supplies
6. Fire (waterproof matches/lighter/candles)
7. Repair kit and tools
8. Nutrition (extra food)
9. Hydration (extra water)
10. Emergency shelter

HIKING POLES
Hiking poles have become very popular and are strongly recommended, as they provide extra stability on uneven ground or downhill and extra leverage when going uphill. They are also invaluable to help with river crossings. Some prefer one pole, others prefer two. The lightweight ones that collapse can be easily tucked into the side of most backpacks. The advice to "never go hiking without your pole(s)" is worth heeding and isn't wimpy!

COMPASS
Learning to use a compass is easy and provides an extra layer of safety when hiking whether the terrain is known

or unknown, as sudden weather changes can obscure or obliterate the most familiar landscapes.

RIVER-CROSSING SAFETY ON GLACIAL STREAMS

Most glacial river crossings on the flanks of Mt Hood Wilderness do not have bridges. Timberline and PCT hikers should be prepared for dangerous river conditions. The following safety procedures are recommended before attempting any river crossing.

- Avoid hiking alone when crossing glacial streams.
- Check the weather before your trip. Avoid these trails if storms are predicted.
- Plan crossings for early morning, when glacial rivers are lower.
- Be willing to turn back if conditions appear unsafe. Red flags include: fast water; difficulty determining depth; very cold temperatures; water higher than your knees; downstream hazards like waterfalls; the sound of boulders rolling along the bottom.
- Scout up and down for the safest crossing, which may not be the trail crossing.
- Look for gradual banks, shallow water free of obstructions, and similar conditions downstream.
- Keep your pack on, but undo the hip and chest strap. Remove the pack if you lose footing.
- Wear boots, sneakers, or water sandals for foot protection and ankle support.
- Use a hiking pole as a 3rd leg, especially on the upstream side and to scout for drop offs.
- Cross together. Face upstream and get in a line perpendicular to the stream's flow. Grab the person's shirt in front of you and move sideways one foot at a time, feeling for a stable surface

before transferring your weight. Two people
can also face each other holding arms and move
sideways (below).

- *Look on the Forest Service website for more river
crossing safety guidelines.*
www.fs.fed.us/r6/mthood

WATER

It is not safe to drink the water from the streams, lakes
and tarns on Mt Hood because many of the streams have
become contaminated. To be on the safe side, carry the
water you need for a day hike (and don't underestimate!)
or take purifying tablets or filter to treat the water.

ANIMALS & BIRDS

About 40 species of mammals
are residents of Mt Hood,
ranging from squirrels, shrews,
pikas, marmots and weasels, to
coyotes, black bear, mountain
lions, deer and elk. Most are
glimpsed very seldom because
they are very shy. Almost 150
species of birds have been
observed around Mt Hood.

BE A RESPONSIBLE HIKER

Due to the increasing effects of climate change, the Mt Hood area is experiencing a change of rainfall and wind patterns. With limited funding the Forest Service is only able to do so much to keep up with Mother Nature. It's up to us to do our part to keep the trails clean and free of garbage and detritus.

ABOUT MT HOOD

Mt Hood, rising 11,235 feet above sea level and 9500 feet above the Hood River Valley, is the tallest peak in Oregon. It is one of a string of volcanoes, stretching from Mt Lassen in northern California to Mt Garibaldi in British Columbia, that were formed by intense friction between the Pacific and American tectonic plates. That is the geological explanation for its magnificent presence. There are other, perhaps more romantic and colorful, explanations.

According to an Indian legend, there was once a great natural bridge spanning the Columbia River, near the town now called Cascade Locks. The land was ruled by the supernaturally powerful sons of the Great Spirit: Pahto to the north of the bridge and Wy'East to the south. The braves fell in love with the same maiden but she could not decide which she preferred. So the braves fought a savage battle for her affection, hurling fire and hot stones at each other across the river and devastating the countryside. The "Bridge of the Gods" collapsed, so angering the Great Spirit that he turned his sons into guardians of the Columbia. Wy'East became Mt Hood and Pahto became Mt Adams. The maiden Looit became Mt St Helens.

According to another legend, Paul Bunyan pitched camp one night six strides east of the falls on the Willamette and uprooted a handful of trees to build a roaring fire. In the morning he covered the embers with a huge pile of rocks and soil and sprinkled on some snow, thereby inadvertently forming Mt Hood.

MAPS

It is essential to have and use a *reasonably updated* map when in the mountains. You should also carry a map in your car that shows the access roads as these can be confusing and not always well signed. Maps are available at many outdoor stores and the U.S. Forest Service Information Centers. Don't be surprised to find that distances given may vary quite widely from map to map and from the mileage that we give. The ones that we have found to be the most useful for the Mt Hood area are the *Mt Hood Area Hiking, Riding & Climbing Map (www.Adventuremaps.net)* and the *National Geographic Map #321: Mount Hood (Mount Hood Wilderness)*. The *Adventure* map doesn't show the newly opened section of the Timberline Trail from Coe Creek to Cloud Cap Inn. The *National Geographic* map shows the original (pre-slide) section of the Timberline Trail. We recommend the Mt Hood Winter Trails map (below) for XC/snowshoe trails.

Other useful maps include:
- *National Geographic #820: Mount Hood (Mt Hood & Willamette National Forests)*
- *Mount Hood Geologic Guide & Recreation Map*
- *Green Trails Maps # 462, 462S*
- *Mt Hood Winter Trails.* Available at Mt Hood Museum & Information Center & local area stores

DRIVING TO MT HOOD

The major access roads to Mt Hood are Hwy 26 from Portland and the west, and I-84 and Hwy 35 from the north. Instructions for finding the trailheads are given for each hike.

AREA MAP OF ROADS

HIKE SUMMARY TABLE

Hike Name	Page	Flowers	Kids	Limited Mobility	Easy	Moderately Strenuous	Strenuous	Very Strenuous
Short Hikes								
Little Zigzag Falls	18	•	•	•	•			
Bald Mountain	20	• • •	•	•		•		
Crosstown Trail	23	•	•	•	•			
Camp Creek Loop	25	•	•		•			
Summit Trail to Ski Bowl	27	•	•	•	•			
Umbrella Falls	29	• • •	•	•	•			
Laurel Hill Chute	31	•	•		•			
Summit Meadow & Pioneer Baby's Grave	34	•	•	•	•			
Trillium Lake Loop	37	• •	•	•	•			
Old Salmon River Trail	39	• •	•	•	•			
Lost Creek Nature Trail	42	•	•	•	•			

Hike	Page
Eureka Peak	44
Veda Lake	47
Mountaineer Loop	51
Silcox Hut Loop	54
Buried Forest Overlook	56
Mid Length Hikes	
Frog Butte & Lower Twin Lake	60
Elk Meadows Trailhead—Umbrella Falls Loop	63
Glacier View Sno-Park to Little Zigzag Falls	66
Mirror Lake & Tom Dick & Harry Viewpoint	69
West Fork Falls	72
Multorpor Mountain Viewpoint	75
West Yellowjacket Loop	77
West Leg Road –Summit Meadow—Still Creek Loop	80

CROSS-COUNTRY/SNOWSHOE SUMMARY TABLE	Page	Distance	Easy	More Difficult	Most Difficult
Timberline Lodge Snowshoe Trail (Marked, east of Lodge)	54	0.25 miles	●		
Crosstown Trail (Marked trail)	23	2.7 miles 1-way	●		
Camp Creek Loop (Marked trail)	25	2.5 miles		●	
Summit Trail (Marked trail)	27	2.1 miles 1-way	●	●	
Enid Lake Loop (Marked trail)	66	1 mile	●		
Glacier View Loop (Marked, snow-covered road & trail)	66	2 miles	●		
Kurt's Konnection (Marked trail)	66	1 mile	●		
West Leg Road to Timberline Lodge (snow-covered road)	*	5.5 miles		●	
Barlow Trail- Summit Meadow–Pioneer Baby's Grave (Marked trail)	34	3 miles round-trip			●
Trillium Lake Loop (marked snow-covered road)	37	4.5 miles		●	
Mud Creek Loop (marked snow-covered road)	*	6 miles			●
West Leg Road–Tie Trail–Summit Meadow–Barlow Trail Loop (Mostly unmarked snow-covered roads & trail)	80	6 miles		●	
West Yellowjacket Trail (unmarked snow-covered roads & trail)	75	5 miles			●
Alpine Trail from Timberline Lodge (XC with care, classified as downhill)	72	3 miles			●
Glade Trail from Timberline Lodge (XC with care, classified as downhill)	*	3 miles			●
Sherar Burn Road (Unmarked snow-covered road)	44	10 miles 1-way		●	
Still Creek Road (Unmarked snow-covered road)	47	12 miles to Rhododendron		●	●

*Trail is not described separately in the text but is shown in the map on page "Map of Cross-Country/Snowshoe Trails" on page 16

MAP OF CROSS-COUNTRY/ SNOWSHOE TRAILS

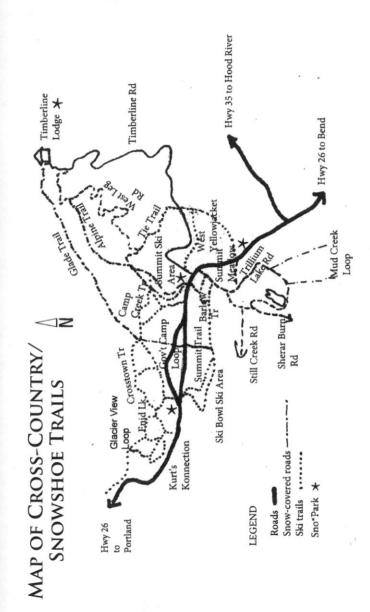

LEGEND

Roads ━━━
Snow-covered roads —·—·—
Ski trails ·······
Sno*Park ★

Short Hikes

Little Zigzag Falls

A jewel of a short hike suitable for all ages, mobility and fitness levels.

DIFFICULTY: Easy, very gentle grade, designed to be wheelchair accessible

DISTANCE: 1 mile round-trip; ½-1 hour

MAPS: Trail #795C. Mt Hood Area Hiking, Riding & Climbing Map, Adventure Maps; National Geographic #321 (Mount Hood Wilderness)

DESCRIPTION: The trail follows the Little Zigzag River and ends at the beautiful Little Zigzag Falls. The falls, though relatively small, are really lovely. The trail is very well maintained, and you'll encounter only a small elevation gain. This is a very peaceful and quiet hike through a beautiful, open forest with the music of the river in the background. Flowers are plentiful in the spring, some mushrooms in the fall.

ACCESS: From Portland, take Hwy 26 east and 4.1 miles after Rhododendron, just after milepost 48, turn *left* (**north**) onto the Kiwanis Camp Rd. (#2639). If driving from Government Camp, take Hwy 26 west for 5.4 miles from the Summit Rest Area at the east end of the Government Camp loop and turn *right* (**north**) onto the Kiwanis Camp Rd. The trailhead is 2.3 miles from Hwy 26, at the end of the paved road, with a porta-potty.

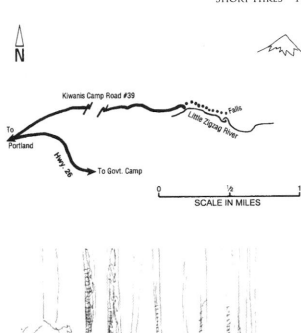

Trail along Little Zigzag River

BALD MOUNTAIN

A "WOW" view of Mt Hood with the hillsides carpeted and ablaze with wildflowers in July & August. The hike from the trailhead is through a magical, open forest with rhododendrons and beargrass flowering in June-July.

DIFFICULTY: Easy, 350–400 feet elevation gain

DISTANCE: 2–3 miles round-trip, or a loop, or hike as long as you want in either direction on the Timberline Trail. If you extend your hike counterclockwise (towards Timberline Lodge), you will reach the Muddy Fork River; ford with care. 1½–3 hours depending on how far you hike

MAP: Trail #785, #600 Mt Hood Area Hiking, Riding & Climbing Map, Adventure Maps; National Geographic #321 (Mount Hood Wilderness)

DESCRIPTION: A short, easy hike suitable for adults at all levels of mobility and fitness and children of all ages. It's an easy uphill through a magical forest (massive expanse of beargrass in early summer) to Bald Mountain with a breathtaking view of Mt Hood, up close and personal, and a stunning mountainside with an extravagant display of alpine flowers in July and early August.

The trail starts at the Top Spur Trailhead and climbs gently for 0.5 mile to a T-junction. Turn *right*, now briefly on the Pacific Crest Trail #2000, signed to Ramona Falls, and walk 100 yards to a 4-way trail junction. ***Be sure to sign in at the Wilderness Permit Box.***

Continue straight, signed Timberline Trail #600, for ~0.25 mile through the forest and emerge dramatically onto the open hillside of Bald Mountain. This is truly a WOW moment. Continue on along and down the trail as long as you want; return the same way or ~0.5 mile from the Wilderness Permit Sign-In Box, when the trail is in the trees, look for a side trail on the *left*, signed Cut-Off Trail, that joins up (in ~100 yards) with the Timberline Trail. Go *left* on the Timberline Trail to return to the 4-way intersection.

ACCESS: From Portland take I-84 **east** to Exit 16, signed to Gresham & Mt Hood, for 2.5 miles; turn *left* (east) onto Hwy 26 (Burnside) & drive 25 miles to Lolo Pass Road (#18). After 4.3 miles, turn *right* onto Rd 1825 for 0.7 mile; just before a bridge, keep straight (instead of crossing the bridge) on a narrow road #1828 for 5.7 miles to a fork. Take the *right* fork for 1.6 miles and find the trailhead on the right. There is usually plenty of parking on the left, opposite the trailhead, but the parking can get very busy on summer weekends— and there is a porta-potty.

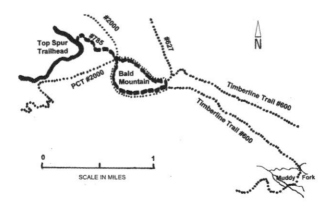

OPTIONAL EXTENSION: once on the Timberline Trail, hike as far as you want in a clockwise or counter-clockwise direction.

Mt Hood vista from Muddy Fork River

Shaggy Mane Mushrooms
(Cuprinus Comatus)

CROSSTOWN TRAIL ❄

A delightful multi-purpose trail that loops to the north of Government Camp and links the Glacier View Sno-Park west of the village with the Summit Ski Area at the east end of the village, accessible from several points in the Government Camp Loop.

DIFFICULTY: Easy, mostly flat with some gentle grades

DISTANCE: 2.7 miles one way, 1½ -2¼ hours; 6 miles round-trip, 3 – 4½ hours

MAPS: Trail #755 Mt Hood Area Hiking, Riding & Climbing Map, Adventure Maps; National Geographic #321 (Mount Hood Wilderness); Mt Hood Winter Trails Map

CAR SHUTTLE: Leave one car at the Glacier View Sno-Park and the other at the Summit Rest Area.

DESCRIPTION: This trail can be hiked one way, with a car shuttle, or as a loop. You can also access it from several places in Government Camp. It is a most welcome addition to the walks and hikes in the Government Camp area, with a section of exquisite forest of second-growth trees mixed with some majestic old-growth. Mt Hood keeps popping up through the trees. Lots of flowers and beargrass bloom in early summer with huckleberries available near Enid Lake in August. This is a perfect XC/ Snowshoe trail for all levels of ability and is close to Government Camp for easy accessibility.

There are two trails linking Crosstown Trail with the Government Camp Loop: Glade Trail (from Timberline

Lodge) and Skiway Trail, cut for a gondola that linked Government Camp and Timberline Lodge. Wally's Tie Trail links the Skiway Trail with the main Crosstown Trail ~0.75 mile from Enid Lake. Look for a large boulder on the downhill side of the trail with a plaque: "In loving memory of Wally, the best damn dog there ever was 1980–90."

ACCESS: 1) *To hike from* **west** *to* **east,** drive 1.5 miles **west** on Hwy 26 from the Summit Rest Area at the east end of the Government Camp business loop and turn *right* onto Rd #552 between mileposts 52 and 53—almost opposite the west entrance to Ski Bowl West. Glacier View Sno-Park, ~200 yards from the highway, offers ample parking. Several trails meet here, so take care to find the right one. Look for the Crosstown Trail sign on the *right* ~50 yards from the parking area and follow the signs to Summit Ski Area.

2) *To hike from* **east** *to* **west,** park at the Summit Rest Area and walk up the service road on the *left* side of the main ski run, behind the Day Lodge, to the point where the power lines cross, just above the last house. Crosstown Trail is clearly marked on a tall pole with sign but is obscured by trees. The start of the trail is 200 yards uphill to the left marked by blue diamonds (cross-country ski trail markers). Follow the signs to Enid Lake or to Glacier View Sno-Park.

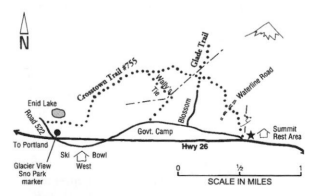

CAMP CREEK LOOP ❄

A short, beautiful forest loop that joins up with Crosstown Trail above Government Camp, crossing picturesque streams on seven bridges.

DIFFICULTY: Easy, ~200 feet elevation gain

DISTANCE: 2.5 miles, 1½ - 2 hours

MAPS: Trail #754 Mt Hood Area Hiking, Riding & Climbing Map, Adventure Maps; National Geographic #321 (Mount Hood Wilderness); Mt Hood Winter Trails Map

DESCRIPTION: Camp Creek Loop is a perfect hike for a hot day as it's mostly shaded. The trail crosses seven small, beautiful streams on sturdy bridges. It's easy to linger and be mesmerized by the water. There aren't many flowers on this hike but the beauty of the streams more than compensates for this. It's also a favorite XC/

Bunchberry

snowshoe trail in winter, very quiet and secluded, and fun to play in the snow by the streams.

ACCESS: *This description of the hike is slightly different from the Forest Service map and description.* The loop can be hiked clockwise or counterclockwise; both start from the Summit Rest Area at the east end of Government Camp by walking up the service road on the left side of the main ski run, behind the Day Lodge, to the point where the power lines cross, just above the last house. If hiking *clockwise,* the sign for the Crosstown Trail is on a tall pole with a sign obscured by trees; the start of the trail is 200 yards uphill to the *left*: follow the blue diamonds. Continue on the trail for ~ 0.5 mile to the signed intersection with the Camp Creek Trail on the *right*. Continue on Camp Creek to its intersection with the Alpine Trail coming down from Timberline Lodge. Turn *right* onto the Alpine Trail and follow it down to the Summit Rest Area.

If hiking *counterclockwise*, continue up the ski area to the top of the chairlift and then onto the Alpine Trail to the *left* of the terminus of the chairlift for ~0.25 mile to a sign for the Camp Creek Trail on the *left*. Follow the trail to a T-junction with the Crosstown Trail and take the *left* arm back to the Summit Rest Area.

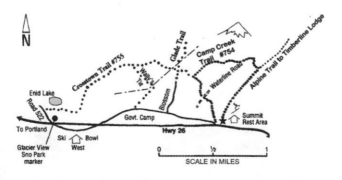

Summit Trail to Ski Bowl

An easy trail along a forest road and trail that links both ends of the Government Camp Loop on the Ski Bowl side of the Loop.

DIFFICULTY: Easy, almost flat service roads

DISTANCE: 2.1 miles each way, 1–1½ hours; 4.2 miles round-trip, 2–3 hours

MAPS: Trail #691 Mt Hood Area Hiking, Riding & Climbing Map, Adventure Maps; National Geographic #321 (Mount Hood Wilderness); Mt Hood Winter Trails Map

DESCRIPTION: The Summit Trail is an easy walk with beautiful views of Mt Hood, magnificent old-growth trees, and flowers along the way. The Adventure Park at Ski Bowl East and Alpine Slide at Ski Bowl may be added attractions. It is also a beautiful and tranquil XC/snowshoe trail in winter. Toilets at Ski Bowl and Summit Rest Area.

From **west** to **east**, park in the large (overflow) parking area at the **east** end of the Ski Bowl West Ski Area loop and look for the sign Summit Trail #691 and Ski Bowl East. Follow this delightful trail through the forest and over Still Creek for 1.25 miles to Ski Bowl East. Continue on the service road, skirting above the Adventure Park at Ski Bowl and the Multorpor Lodge (Food Court and restrooms) and find the service road that continues in the same direction for almost 1 mile to Hwy 26.

From **east to west**: Cross Hwy 26 (carefully) and follow the service road that takes off opposite the Summit Rest Area and continues as a forest road. Follow this for almost a mile to the Adventure Park at Ski Bowl and Multorpor Lodge with a food court and restrooms (Ski Bowl East Ski Area in the winter). Skirt above and around the Lodge, and find the service road below the ski lifts, now called Lake Rd/Summit Trail #691. Just past the last chairlift, Summit Trail takes off to the *right* as a forest trail through beautiful hemlock trees for 1.25 miles, ending at a large (overflow) parking area at the east end of the Ski Bowl West loop.

ACCESS: The hike can be done one-way with a car shuttle or round-trip. For a round-trip, west to east may be easier as there is ample parking by Ski Bowl and you don't need to cross Hwy 26. For west to east, park in a large (overflow) parking lot at the east end of the Ski Bowl Ski Area loop. For east to west, park in the Summit Rest Area at the east end of Government Camp and cross Hwy 26 (carefully).

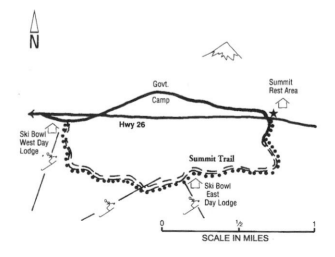

UMBRELLA FALLS

A perfect walk or short hike through a forest of wild-flowers and meadows to a dramatic falls.

DIFFICULTY: Easy, flat

DISTANCE: 0.25 mile, 1 hour to allow time to gaze at the falls

MAPS: Trail #667 Mt Hood Area Hiking, Riding & Climbing Map, Adventure Maps; National Geographic #321 (Mount Hood Wilderness)

DESCRIPTION: This is the ideal walk for the guests from out of town as it combines so much of what is special in Oregon: close-up views of Mt Hood, meadows bursting with wildflowers, and the dramatic Umbrella Falls— possibly even a few deer in the meadow. It's all hard to top.

ACCESS: Continue past Government Camp on Hwy 26, heading **east**, and at the first major junction 2.2 miles past the Summit Rest Area at the far (**east**) end of the Government Camp Loop, take the Hood River exit, which is Hwy 35. Continue on Hwy 35 for 6.8 miles to the Mt Hood Meadows Ski Area access road on the *right*. The Umbrella Trail crosses the road in another 1.5 miles (0.2 mile before the main Mt Hood Meadows Ski Area parking lot) and may be hard to spot. Look for the trailhead signs

Columbine

on the *right side* of the road, just below road level, and park on the shoulder. The trail starts down the bank.

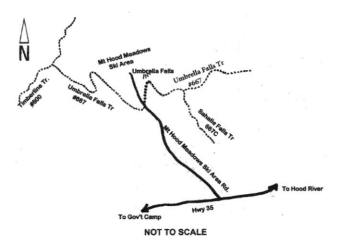

NOT TO SCALE

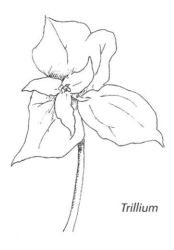

Trillium

LAUREL HILL CHUTE TRAIL

A site where ropes were used to winch the loaded wagons down a steep slope, giving us a glimpse into one of the many hardships of the Oregon Trail.

DIFFICULTY: Easy, 200 feet elevation gain, gentle grade

DISTANCE: 1 mile round-trip; ¾-1 hour

MAP: Trail #795A Mt Hood Area Hiking, Riding & Climbing Map, Adventure Maps; National Geographic #321 (Mount Hood Wilderness)

DESCRIPTION: A short trail that climbs to the top of Laurel Hill—reputedly the section of the historic Barlow Wagon Trail where the pioneers had to ease their wagons down a steep, rocky chute by braking their descent with ropes wound around trees. The trail is well marked and well graded. The history adds flavor to the hike, and the views are worth the short climb.

From Hwy 26, the trail climbs up to the old highway by a flight of steps, follows the road to the *right* past an interesting interpretive plaque, then takes off on the *left* and climbs 0.4 mile in gentle loops, passing two forks—both on the right. Ignore both of them. At the second fork, continue straight, ignoring the downhill shortcut trail on the left, to reach the top of the chute. Return by the same trail (don't use shortcuts as they erode the trails). Accessibility and historic interest have made this a popular trail, but there is usually room to park at the trailhead.

There is some controversy about whether the rocky chute at Laurel Hill was really the site of the infamous, precipitous chute, so feared by the pioneers because of the toll it took on wagons and livestock. Whether or not it is the exact site, this short hike gives a fascinating glimpse into the past, and makes the feats of the pioneers all the more impressive. The views down the Zigzag valley, towards

*Wagons being
winched down Laurel Hill*

Clintonia

Portland, are superb. The name Laurel comes from the rhododendrons that belong to the laurel family and grow in abundance in the area.

ACCESS: The trailhead is on the **south** side of Hwy 26, 6.4 miles **east** of Rhododendron. If you are driving **west** from Government Camp, you have to drive 4.1 miles **west,** turn around at the Kiwanis Camp Road and drive back to the parking. The parking area is small but usually adequate and is well marked by an historical site sign.

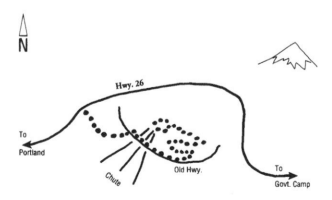

NOT TO SCALE

SUMMIT MEADOW & PIONEER BABY'S GRAVE ❄

A very easy hike on parts of the historic Barlow Wagon Trail to a meadow where the pioneers wintered over.

DIFFICULTY: Easy, 200 feet elevation gain

DISTANCE: 3 miles round-trip, 1½ - 2 hours

MAPS: Trail #601A & Still Creek Rd. Mt Hood Area Hiking, Riding & Climbing Map, Adventure Maps; maps of Gov't Camp winter & summer trails available at the Museum & Information Center in Gov't Camp

DESCRIPTION: A delightful, easy hike partly on the Historic Barlow Wagon Trail, partly on a paved forest road. The goal of the hike is the beautiful Summit Meadow where the pioneers and their livestock rested before pushing on to the difficult stretch to the west. The portion of the hike on the paved Still Creek Road provides access to Still Creek Campground and Trillium Lake, so watch out for cars. Also a delightful XC/snowshoe trail in winter. : the Hemlock Trail is Easy; the Barlow Trail is More Difficult.

ACCESS: Park at the Summit Rest Area at the east end of the Government Camp business loop, cross Hwy 26 (carefully) and find a service road at a brown sign for Timberline Lodge. Follow the service road for 50 yards to a primitive road on the *left* (look for the blue diamond cross-country ski trail markers on the trees). Follow the cross-country ski trail for ~100 yards, passing signage for the Barlow Trail and Summit Meadow (behind the Forest Service cabins). After ~ 100 yards, the trail passes along the top of a cut through the trees where there is a sign for Hemlock Trail to the *left* (cross-country ski trail in winter). Keep *straight on* (now the Barlow Trail), re-enter the forest, and ignore a side trail that joins the main trail from the right. Continue on gently downhill for ~0.5 mile until you cross Still Creek and join the paved road

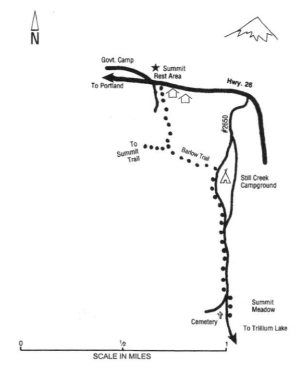

through Still Creek Campground. Turn *right* onto the paved road and follow it through the campground—the road becomes Perry Vickers Rd—and on to Summit Meadow. The paving ends just after the campground and the road passes several private cabins. At the beginning of the meadow, there is a 3-way junction. To find the Pioneer Baby's grave, keep going straight: the grave is a few yards further, on the *right*, and is fenced.

Just before the junction, opposite the Pioneer Baby's Grave (1882), there is an information board (Tele Tales) that gives a phone number (503–342–3597, 21#) to hear the history of Summit Meadow in the late 1880s. Return the same way.

OPTION FOR THOSE WITH LIMITED MOBILITY: Drive down to Summit Meadow, check out Pioneer Baby's Grave, listen to the Tele-Tales & imagine you are back on the Barlow Trail in your wagon in the late 1880s.

TRILLIUM LAKE LOOP ❄

A 1.9 mile loop around Trillium Lake that offers fantastic views of Mt Hood. Perfect for a short hike with the whole family and for those with limited mobility. A longer XC/snowshoeing trail in winter as the access roads to Trillium Lake are closed.

DIFFICULTY: Easy, flat & excellent trail, designed to be barrier free

DISTANCE: 1.9 miles, 1- 1½ hours

MAPS: Trail #761 Mt Hood Area Hiking, Riding & Climbing Map, Adventure Maps; National Geographic #321 (Mount Hood Wilderness)

DESCRIPTION: *This trail was designed to be barrier free*, with a forest trail surface or wooden boardwalk, and works very well for kids, strollers and those with limited mobility. It has become a favorite of the family as it provides a perfect opportunity to mix time on and in Trillium Lake with an easy hike with fabulous views of Mt Hood, flowers, and trees for hide-and-seek. Swimming and fishing are popular things to do here and there is a large campground beside the lake and a day use area with shelter. The trail crosses wetlands at the far end of the loop.

Trillium Lake Boardwalk

From the parking area just before the dam, cross the dam and find the start of the trail on the *right*. From then on, just follow the trail around the end of the lake. There are only two places where you need to make a decision: after the trail loops around the top of the lake, and when returning towards the dam. The first is a fork where the boardwalk has an extension to the *right* for a photo op, so keep *left*; the second is another fork with the *left* arm being a bike trail, so stay *right*. The trail passes the campground, an amphitheater and two boat ramps. Toilets are available in the campground.

CROSS-COUNTRY/SNOWSHOEING: XC skiing & snowshoeing in the Trillium Basin is incredible as the trails are usually tracked for XC skiing on weekends by volunteers (boxes for donations at trailheads). Access is from Sno-Park at Summit Ski Area via Still Creek Rd or Snowbunny Sno-Park via Trillium Lake Loop Rd. See "Map of Cross-Country/Snowshoe Trails" on page 16.

ACCESS: From Government Camp head **east** on Hwy 26 for 2 miles and turn *right* onto the Trillium Lake Loop Road (Forest Rd #2656) for 1.8 miles to the dam where there is parking (*need permit*) and access to the lake. Access also via the other exits to the Trillium Lake Campground.

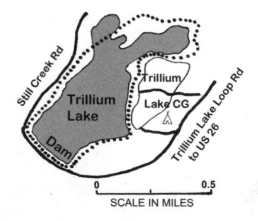

SCALE IN MILES

OLD SALMON RIVER TRAIL

A very accessible trail along the Salmon River through a cathedral-like forest with old-growth trees.

DIFFICULTY: Easy, mostly flat, well maintained trail

DISTANCE: 2.4 miles one way with car shuttle, 1½ - 1¾ hours; 4.8 miles round-trip, 3 - 3½ hours

MAPS: Trail #742A Mt Hood Area Hiking, Riding & Climbing Map, Adventure Maps; National Geographic #321 (Mount Hood Wilderness)

DESCRIPTION: The Old Salmon River Trail provides one of the most accessible opportunities to see the majesty of old-growth trees. This is a mature forest so there are trees at all stages of growth—a superb place to see "nurse" logs overgrown with mosses, ferns, and ground cover, and sprouting shrubs and trees. The river provides an attraction equal to the forest, and is within sight for most of the trail. The trail is excellent and, after the short steep descent to the river, has virtually no elevation gain or loss, so it is suitable for the whole family and the proximity to the river is appealing to kids. The trail follows the Salmon River for the whole length, joining the road briefly for two segments. The trail ends at a bridge over the Salmon River and continues on the east (*left*) side of the road as the Salmon River Trail.

CAR SHUTTLE: Leave one car at the bridge over the Salmon River, ~2.4 miles from the trailhead, and the other at the trailhead.

ACCESS: The trailhead is on the Old Salmon River Road, off Hwy 26 at Wemme. From Portland, take Hwy 26 **east** towards Mt Hood. From Government Camp, take Hwy 26 **west** towards Portland. At Wemme turn **south** at the traffic light by the Hoodland Plaza shopping

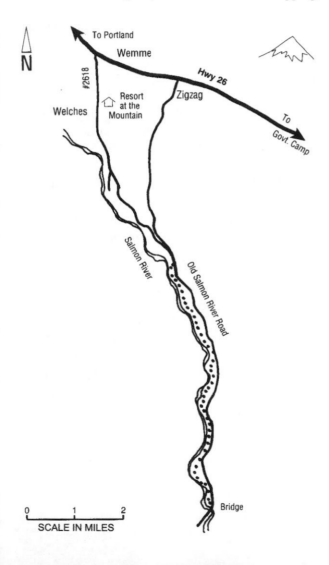

center onto Welches Road (Rd #2618); continue on this road for 2.4 miles, passing The Resort at the Mountain and keeping left at the Y-junction at 2 miles, until you meet the Old Salmon River Road. Turn *right* onto the Old Salmon River Road. The trailhead is on the *right*, 0.7 mile past the junction, and is marked by a sign "The Old Salmon River Trail." There is usually ample parking on the right, beside the trailhead, and a porta-potty.

Old Salmon River Trail

LOST CREEK NATURE TRAIL

An easy, flat, mostly paved trail through a beautiful grove of trees with interesting interpretive plaques that provide information about the area's flora, fauna, and geography.

DIFFICULTY: Easy, flat, wheelchair accessible

DISTANCE: 0.5 mile loop, ½ hour at leisurely pace

MAPS: National Geographic #321 (Mount Hood Wilderness)

DESCRIPTION: The Lost Creek Nature Trail was built by volunteers in 1972 to make an outdoor experience accessible to all. Benches are placed strategically and conveniently along the trail, as are wheelchair-accessible toilets. This is an ideal short, easy trail suitable for young children as well as those who are less mobile. The trail, shaped like a keyhole, is easy to follow and winds through the trees, round to viewpoints over the creek, and by beaver ponds. The short section that is unpaved has a broad, sturdy wooden boardwalk.

Lost Creek Nature Trail

The interpretive plaques explain how, in part from a mudflow from Mt Hood over 200 years ago, nature has formed this beautiful spot. The majestic trees, lichens, lush mosses and ferns convey a special atmosphere. This is a lovely trail to introduce children to the beauty of the outdoors. They may particularly enjoy looking at the "nurse" logs—portions of fallen trees that are nurturing the growth of new plants and trees. The drive to the trailhead is also attractive with moss covering the rocks, banks, and forest floor. There is a very pleasant campground beside the trail.

ACCESS: From Portland take I-84 east to Exit 16, signed to Gresham & Mt Hood, and after 2.5 miles, turn *left* (**east**) onto Hwy 26 (Burnside) for 25 miles then turn *left* (**north**) onto Lolo Pass Road (Rd #18). Continue on Rd #18 for 4.1 miles. Turn *right* onto paved Rd #1825, drive 0.7 mile, turn *right* across a bridge and drive 1.1 miles to a fork. Take the *right* fork onto Rd #1825–100, signed to Burnt Lake trailhead and Lost Creek Campground, for 0.3 mile to another fork: the *right* fork leads to Lost Creek Campground. The parking for the Lost Creek Nature Trail is 0.3 mile from the fork, through the campground.

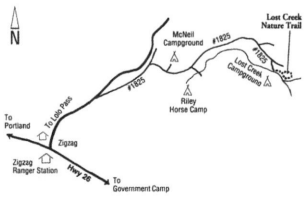

NOT TO SCALE

Eureka Peak

A perfect hike when the wild rhododendrons and beargrass are blooming, usually mid-June to early July.

DIFFICULTY: Moderately Strenuous, 1000 feet elevation gain

DISTANCE: 2.4 miles round-trip, 1½-2 hours

MAPS: Trail #671 Mt Hood Area Hiking, Riding & Climbing Map, Adventure Maps; National Geographic #321 (Mount Hood Wilderness)

DESCRIPTION: The Eureka Peak Trail is a very quiet, peaceful hike that is relatively unknown. Soon after leaving the trailhead, the trail crosses a pretty stream (look for a good crossing), and makes one zig before heading relatively straight up the hill to link two unpaved roads, Still Creek Road and Sherar Burn Road. There are a few relatively steep pitches, but mostly the trail has a comfortable grade. Eureka Peak can be seen through the trees to the north-east.

The hike can be extended by walking in either direction along Sherar Burn Road at the south end of the trail. The Sherar Burn Road trailhead for Eureka Peak trail is not well-marked, however. Take a good bearing so you don't miss the entrance. The musical sound of the stream can be heard for the first part of the trail. Also listen for the liquid song of the thrush and the whirr of the mountain grouse. Wildflowers abound in late June and July—bunchberries, lupine, anemones, columbine, wild strawberries, paintbrush, clintonia, penstemon, and

Washington Lilies. The forest is pleasantly open with mixed conifers including Douglas-fir, Western Hemlock, White Pine, Lodgepole Pine, and cedar.

ACCESS: From the Summit Rest Area at the east end of the Government Camp business loop, go **east** on Hwy 26 for 0.2 mile and take the Mt Hood National Forest Still Creek Campground exit on the *right* (Rd #2650). The road loops through the campground—keep straight when it loops back—and continues to a large open meadow, Summit Meadow, ~1 mile from Hwy 26. The paved road ends just after the campground. Near the beginning of the meadow, at a junction, take the *right*

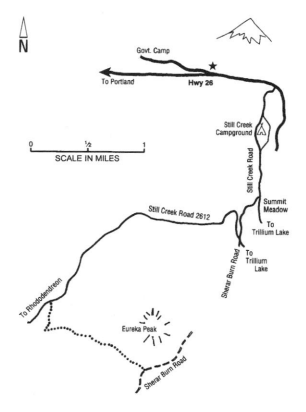

(***west***) fork (E. Chimney Rock Road) and continue to a
4-way intersection after 0.4 mile. Take the first (sharp)
right road, signed to Rhododendron (Still Creek Rd
#2612) and follow this for 2.4 miles on a crushed rock
road with some potholes. The trailhead takes off from
the ***left*** (south) side of the road. It is not obvious, but is
clearly marked by a trailhead sign ~30 feet in from the
road. Watch your odometer and you won't go wrong.

OPTIONAL ADD-ON: This hike can be made longer
by combining it with the Veda Lake Trail (page 47).
To do this, turn ***right*** when you reach the Sherar Burn
Road and hike to the Veda Lake Trailhead (~2 miles). Be
sure to mark the Eureka Peak Trailhead so you can find
it when you return!

Washington Lilies

VEDA LAKE

*A beautiful trail to an attractive small lake suitable
for swimming and fishing. It's likely to be deserted
as the access road is very rutted with giant potholes:
a sporting adventure that demands a vehicle with
high clearance.*

DIFFICULTY: Moderately Strenuous 800 feet elevation gain

DISTANCE: 2.4 miles round-trip, 1½ - 2½ hours

MAPS: Trail #673 Mt Hood Area Hiking, Riding &
Climbing Map, Adventure Maps; National Geographic
#321 (Mount Hood Wilderness)

DESCRIPTION: This is a great hike for those seeking
solitude as the terrible access road limits the number of
people who can get to the trailhead. The trail begins on the
right (north) side of the road, across from the parking area
and is signed to Veda Lake. The trail is well maintained and
well-graded and starts with a modest uphill grade, levels
out, then drops in gentle zigzags to the lake. Most of the
elevation gain is on the return as
the trail climbs back from the lake.
This trail offers a few great views of
Mt Hood, a beautiful open mixed
forest and plentiful wildflowers:
lupine, paintbrush, twinflower,
penstemon, Washington Lilies,
bunchberries, and rhododendrons.
The 3-acre lake has become the
home to Eastern Brook trout since
Vern Rogers and Dave Donaldson

Washington Lily

introduced them in 1917 (the name Veda comes from the combination of their first names). Enjoy a swim before heading back up the trail. A great site for camping, picnicking, fishing, and swimming; mushrooms in the fall.

ACCESS: From the Summit Rest Area at the east end of the Government Camp business loop, go **east** on Hwy 26 to the first intersection on the *right*, 0.2 mile from the Rest Area, signed to the Mt Hood National Forest Still Creek Campground (Rd #2650). The road loops through the campground and continues to a large open meadow, Summit Meadow, ~1 mile from Hwy 26. The paved road ends at the end of the campground. Near the beginning of the meadow, at a 3-way junction, take the *right* fork (E. Chimney Rock Rd) and continue to a 4-way intersection after 0.4 mile. Keep *straight ahead* on the Sherar Burn Rd #2613. This road begins with a fairly good surface but soon deteriorates and becomes narrow, rocky and rutted with giant potholes. Only vehicles with high clearance should be tempted though some Subaru drivers accept the challenge! The trailhead and parking is 3.5 miles up the Sherar Burn Rd, on the *left* at the Fir Tree Campground.

Arnica

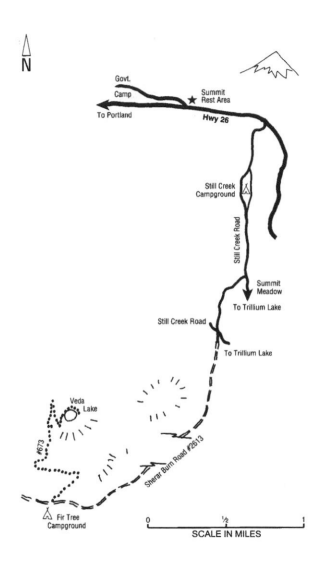

Timberline Lodge

Timberline Lodge provides a convenient starting point for many hikes. Parking is easy. The main lodge and Wy'east Day Lodge offer a range of options for refreshments, plus a gift shop and ski rental area. Timberline Lodge itself is a remarkable and impressive building and well worth a visit.

Built in the mid-1930s as a project of the Works Progress Administration, it has been lovingly maintained and restored by the US Forest Service, Friends of Timberline, and the RLK Corporation. It is a wonderful place to stay or just to linger and enjoy the ambience. The handcrafted furnishings are perfectly suited to the Lodge and its setting, and the views in every direction are stunning. Function, art and whimsy combine to make the inside of the Lodge striking. The staircase newel posts are carved in the form of a variety of animals that invite you to touch and fondle them.

Newel Posts

SHORT HIKES FROM TIMBERLINE LODGE

MOUNTAINEER LOOP
(SHORTER, LOWER PORTION)

A 2-part hike that includes a short, easy loop from Timberline Lodge, suitable for adults with limited mobility, all fitness levels, and kids of all ages, and a longer loop that climbs up to the Silcox Hut (described separately). There is a generous carpet of alpine flowers in both loops with the flowers in the Silcox loop dwarfed by the altitude and exposure.

DIFFICULTY: Easy, very little elevation gain or loss

DISTANCE: 2 miles for loop, 1–1½ hours

MAPS: Trail #798 Mt Hood Area Hiking, Riding & Climbing Map, Adventure Maps; National Geographic #321 (Mount Hood Wilderness)

DESCRIPTION: The Mountaineer Trail works well as a short loop from Timberline Lodge suitable for all ages or as a more challenging and longer loop with 1000 feet elevation gain (see Silcox Hut Loop, page 54). The views in every direction are stunning and the wildflowers in July and August are gorgeous. Remnants of snow in the gullies in early summer give the kids a chance to slide or throw snowballs!

The Mountaineer Trail can either be hiked *clockwise or counterclockwise* from the lodge. To hike *clockwise* turn *right* coming out of the main lodge doors and follow the paved road that passes above the bottom of the Magic Mile Chairlift. Where the road forks, just past the lift, take the *left* fork (Mountaineer Trail) and immediately look for a sign for the PCT at the far end of a small parking area for service vehicles. The Mountaineer Trail and the Timberline Trail/PCT join after 0.6 mile. Turn *right* on the Timberline Trail/PCT to return to the lodge.

To hike *counterclockwise,* turn *left* coming out of the main lodge doors, find a paved service road on the *left* and follow it up a short distance to where the combined Timberline Trail/Pacific Crest Trail (PCT) cross the service road. Turn *left* onto this trail, follow it for ~0.5 mile, and turn *left* onto the Mountaineer Trail back to the Lodge.

OPTIONAL ADD ON: Do the whole Mountaineer Loop by continuing on to the upper part of the Loop. See the

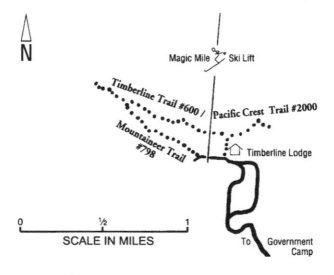

Silcox Hut Loop, page 54. The upper loop takes off from the junction of the PCT/Timberline Trail and the lower part of the Mountaineer Loop, or from Timberline Lodge.

ACCESS: From the Summit Rest Area at the far (east) end of the Government Camp business loop, take Hwy 26 **east** for 0.25 miles, turn *left* onto Timberline Road, and drive 6 miles to the parking areas for Timberline Lodge.

Volcanic History of Mt Hood

Recent eruptions: 1804, 1853, 1854, 1859, 1865, 1907

Mt Hood is one of a string of volcanoes forming the Cascade Range and stretching from Mt Lassen in California to Mt Garibaldi in British Columbia. The Cascade volcanoes erupt far less frequently than the Hawaiian volcanoes, but their proximity to populated areas make them potentially more dangerous.

The Cascade volcanoes are composite volcanoes, have steep sides, and erupt magma that is very sticky. The expanding gases can't escape easily from the sticky magma and build up pressure, leading to explosive eruptions. The Hawaiian volcanoes are shield volcanoes, so called because their long sloping sides look like an inverted warrior's shield.

Lewis and Clark, in 1805, saw some of the effects of an eruption which was probably in the early 1790s. They described a river (the Sandy) that was essentially choked with sandy sediment, much like the Toutle River after the eruption of Mt St Helens in 1980.

Mt Hood's eruptions have mostly been characterized by lava flows and dome-building and dome-collapsing, rather than very explosive. The most recent period of eruptions was centered at Crater Rock, ~700 feet below the summit, and involved pyroclastic flows of gas, rock and ash, and mudslides primarily involving the mountain's south side.

No one knows when Mt Hood will erupt again, but erupt it will - almost certainly.

SILCOX HUT LOOP ❄

(UPPER PART OF THE MOUNTAINEER TRAIL)

A short but moderately strenuous hike from Timberline Lodge up to the Silcox Hut, built in 1939 as the upper terminus for Timberline Lodge's original Magic Mile ski lift.

DIFFICULTY: Moderately Strenuous, 1000 feet elevation gain from Timberline Lodge. For an **Easy** walk, follow any of the well-marked trails behind the Lodge.

DISTANCE: 2 miles round-trip, 1½-2 hours

MAPS: Trail #798 Mt Hood Area Hiking, Riding & Climbing Map, Adventure Maps; National Geographic #321 (Mount Hood Wilderness)

DESCRIPTION: The Silcox Hut is located 1000 feet above Timberline Lodge, close to the terminus of the Magic Mile ski run. The hike is moderately steep but not difficult and rewards the hiker with spectacular views up to Mt Hood and south to Trillium Lake, Mt Jefferson, Three Sisters and Broken Top. The predominant flowers on the mountainside are lupine, dwarfed by the altitude.

Turn *left* coming out of the main Lodge doors, find a paved service road on the *left* and follow it up a short distance to where the combined Timberline Trail/PCT cross the service road; turn *right* onto this trail. Continue on, cross a shallow gully, and look for the Mountaineer Trail #798 (also called the Silcox Hut Trail) heading uphill on your *left*. Follow this up to the Silcox Hut. Return the same way or loop back to the Lodge by following the service road or any of the social paths that head downwards. The views in every direction are stunning. There is a short snowshoe trail to the east of the Lodge.

ACCESS: From the Summit Rest Area at the far (**east**) end of the Government Camp business loop, take Hwy 26 **east** for 0.25 mile, turn *left* onto Timberline Road, and drive 6 miles to the parking areas for Timberline Lodge.

SKI LIFT OPTION: In summer, you can take the Magic Mile Ski Lift up (and down).

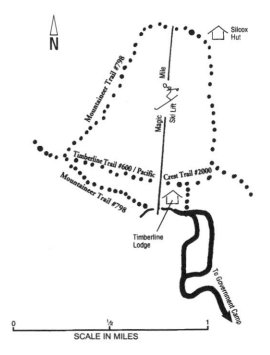

BURIED FOREST OVERLOOK

This short hike from Timberline Lodge offers the chance to see the remains of a forest buried by the last eruption of Mt Hood over 200 years ago and the rocky moraines left behind by the glaciers that scoured the mountain.

DIFFICULTY: Easy, very little elevation gain

DISTANCE: 1.2 miles round-trip, 1 hour

MAPS: Trails #600, #2000 Mt Hood Area Hiking, Riding & Climbing Map, Adventure Maps; National Geographic #321 (Mount Hood Wilderness)

DESCRIPTION: A short, easy hike to the Buried Forest Overlook that is suitable for adults at all levels of fitness and children of all ages. The starkness of the White River Canyon contrasts with the colorful beauty of the wildflowers that carpet the mountainside beside the trail in season.

ACCESS: Turn *left* as you exit Timberline Lodge main entrance and immediately find a paved service road on the *left* going up the mountain. Follow it the short distance to where the Timberline Trail (#600) and the Pacific Crest Trail (PCT, #2000) cross the service road. Turn *right* (**east**) and continue on the combined Timberline Trail/ PCT for 0.6 mile to the White River Canyon Overlook on a spur to the *left* of the main trail.

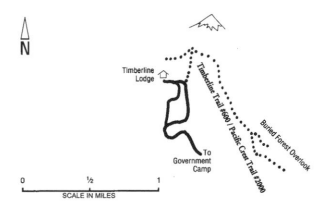

Riding a bicycle down Mt Hood?

In 1946, Ty Kearney had the unusual idea of taking a bike up to the summit and riding it down! So, in 1947, he and a group of his friends carried a bicycle up to the summit in pieces, re-assembled it, and took turns riding it down. Not surprisingly, pedaling was very challenging because of the soft snow and pumice sand, but they did it!

The Mazamas mountaineering club was organized on the summit of Mt Hood on July 19, 1894. One party climbed from Cloud Cap on the north side, but most toiled up from Portland and Government Camp. The weather was most inhospitable that day, with thunder and sleet, and a hundred climbers turned back. 155 men and 38 women made it to the top and the Mazamas was born.

Mid-Length Hikes

FROG BUTTE & LOWER TWIN LAKE LOOP

A moderately strenuous loop through beautiful and changing forest with views of Mt Hood from the top of Frog Butte, and a chance to swim or fish in Lower Twin Lake.

DIFFICULTY: Moderately Strenuous, 1,500 feet elevation gain

DISTANCE: 7.0 mile loop, 4- 5 hours

MAPS: Trails #530, #484, #495, #2000 Mt Hood Area Hiking, Riding & Climbing Map, Adventure Maps; National Geographic #321 (Mount Hood Wilderness)

DESCRIPTION: This lovely loop hike joins up several trails: Frog Lake Trail #530, Frog Lake Butte Trail #484, Twin Lakes Trail #495, and a portion of the Pacific Crest Trail #2000. The trail climbs steadily from the trailhead to the top of Frog Butte, then drops gently to Lower Twin Lake. The trails are all well maintained and easy to follow.

From the trailhead, the trail climbs at an easy grade, crosses a clear-cut and the forest road up to Frog Butte, and continues up (at a much steeper grade) for 1.5 miles to a T-junction. To continue to the top of Frog Butte, turn *right* (#530) and continue to climb quite steeply for another 0.75 mile to a rough road that winds round to the summit. Turn *right* and follow this road to the top of the butte. Depending on the time you have available, the side trail to the top of Frog Butte may be worth a miss because new growth in the clear-cut has blocked out some (but not all) of the previously spectacular view of Mt Hood. To continue to Lower Twin Lake, return to the T-junction and go *straight* for 1.5 miles until the trail reaches Lower Twin Lake with campsites at the north end. The trail takes off at the NE corner of the lake and joins a trail coming in from the *right* from Upper Twin Lake. Turn *left*, signed to Wapinitia Pass 2 miles, and climb gradually back above the lake and down to meet the Pacific Crest Trail (#2000) at a T-junction. Take the *left* fork, signed to Wapinitia Pass, for 1.5miles to the large parking area. Either take the trail just before the parking area, signed Frog Lake 0.5 mile, or cross the parking area. Both will lead to the road to Frog Lake Campground and back to your car.

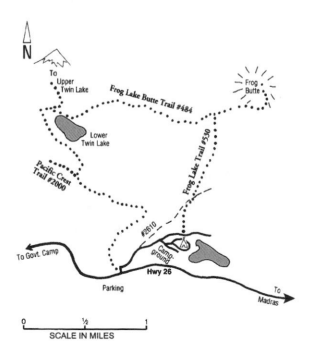

ACCESS: From the Summit Rest Area at the **east** end of the Government Camp business loop, drive **east** on Hwy 26. At 2.2 miles, the road divides with Hwy 35 to Hood River taking off to the *right* and Hwy 26 continuing *straight*. Stay on Hwy 26 for another 6.9 miles and turn into a large parking area on the *left* side of the highway, signed to Frog Lake Campground. Follow the campground road for 0.4 mile to a fork. The *right* fork goes to the campground.

Continue straight for another 0.2 mile to the unsigned trailhead on the *left* side of the road. Parking is available beside the road.

Lower Twin Lake

ELK MEADOWS TRAILHEAD— UMBRELLA FALLS LOOP

A relatively easy loop hike that rewards the hiker with splashy displays of alpine flowers, pretty flower-edged streams, quiet forest and two dramatic waterfalls.

DIFFICULTY: Moderately Strenuous, 857 feet elevation gain if hiked counterclockwise from the Elk Meadows Trailhead

DISTANCE: 4.4 miles for the loop, 2½-3 hours

MAP: Trails #645, #667, #667C Mt Hood Area Hiking, Riding & Climbing Map, Adventure Maps; National Geographic #321 (Mount Hood Wilderness)

DESCRIPTION: This favorite hike has the winning combination of hillsides packed with wildflowers, dramatic views of Mt Hood and picturesque waterfalls. Most reasonably fit adults and children who can hike 4-5 miles and 900 feet elevation gain can easily do this. The loop works either clockwise (heading west towards Timberline Lodge) or counterclockwise (heading northeast). The counterclockwise direction (described below) probably wins by a nose.

The loop starts at the Elk Meadows Trailhead where there is an information board with signage to Elk Meadows Trail #645 and Umbrella Falls Trail #667, and a porta-potty.

To hike counterclockwise, take the Elk Meadows Trail #645 from the parking area for ~0.4 mile (ignoring a trail that joins the main trail soon after the start of the trail coming in from the ski area parking) and turn *left* at a trail junction signed Umbrella Falls Trail #667. This trail climbs quite steeply then levels out, crosses some of the Mt Hood Meadows Ski Area runs and reaches a T-Junction after 1.3 miles. Turn *right* for ~0.3 mile to the beautiful Umbrella Falls.

To return, backtrack to the T-junction and continue *straight*, now on the Sahalie Falls Trail #667C. The trail descends through the forest at a gentle grade for 1.6 miles and merges onto a road that leads to a viewpoint for the Sahalie Falls (*right* when you reach the paved road). Towards the end of the trail (before you reach the paved road) there is an option to take a somewhat precipitous trail to view the falls. It's better (and safer) to wait until you can go to see the falls on the paved road! Once you reach the paved road, either take the continuation of the trail directly across the road to return to the Elk Meadows Trailhead parking or follow the road left to the parking area.

Stream on Umbrella Falls Trail

To hike clockwise, either find the start of the Sahalie Falls Trail #667C on the opposite side of the road from the parking area or follow the paved road around to the *left* and find the start of the trail on the mountain *(right)* side of the road. The trail climbs gently through quiet forest. Soon after the beginning of the trail, there is a side trail to the *left* that leads to a viewpoint over Sahalie Falls (note caution above). The main trail reaches a T-junction after 1.6 miles. Keep *straight on* for ~0.3 mile to the beautiful Umbrella Falls, then backtrack to the T-junction and take the *left* fork onto the Umbrella Falls Trail #667 for 1.3 miles to a T-junction with the Elk Meadows Trail #645. Turn *right* for the 0.4 mile to the parking area.

ACCESS: From Government Camp, drive 2.2 miles to the junction of Hwy 26 & 35, take the exit to Hwy 35 and drive **north** (towards Hood River) for 7.9 miles to the Elk Meadows Trailhead signed to the *left*. The trailhead is <0.25 mile on the *right* with ample parking and a porta-potty.

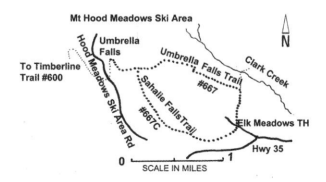

Glacier View Sno-Park to Little Zigzag Falls ❄

*An easy trail, through a beautiful, open and lush
forest with abundant huckleberry bushes (berries in
mid-August) to a truly magical stream and waterfall. Perfect for a hot day. Trail bikes are a potential
hazard for hikers.*

DIFFICULTY: Easy, gentle grades, ~400 feet elevation
gain

DISTANCE: 4.5 miles round-trip, 3-4½ hours

MAPS: Trails #795, #795C Mt Hood Area Hiking,
Riding & Climbing Map, Adventure Maps; National
Geographic #321 (Mount Hood Wilderness)

DESCRIPTION: This gentle hike along segments of
the historic Barlow Wagon Trail and the old Mt Hood
highway combines two trails, Pioneer Bridle Trail #795
and Little ZigZag Trail #795C. The Little Zigzag Trail is
a jewel of a short hike (see description page 18) along
the lovely Zigzag River, ending up at a beautiful falls that
make a surprising and delightful destination for the hike.
The forest changes constantly in character throughout
the hike as the amount of water varies. Wildflowers,
rhododendrons, moss and birds abound. Huckleberries
are abundant around Enid Lake in August.

The trail can be easily seen from the Sno-Park. Follow
the trail to the *left (west)* and where it divides (~100
yards), take the *right* fork, signed Pioneer Bridle Trail and
marked with blue diamond-shaped ski trail signs high on

the trees. Continue gently downhill, past a junction on the *right* after ~0.3 mile, signed Enid Lake Ski Trail & Crosstown Trail, and a junction on the *left* that leads up to the old highway after another 0.5 mile. The trail then drops steadily in loops and comes very close to Hwy 26. Continue on until the trail goes through a tunnel under the old highway (watch carefully for the trail to the tunnel on the *left*)—at this point you can see the old paved highway on the *right*. Take the old highway to the *right* for ~0.25 mile and find the trailhead to Little Zigzag Falls on the *right*, just after a barrier. Porta-potty at start of Little Zigzag Trail. Return the same way.

Parts of this hike are linked to the Enid Lake Loop and Glacier View Loop XC/Snowshoe Trails—see map page 16.

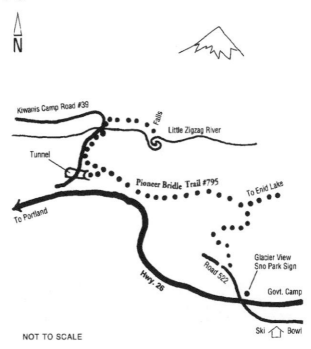

NOT TO SCALE

Unlike the Forest Service's named and numbered hikes this is a composite of portions of two hikes; so some care is needed in following the map and instructions. *Watch out for bikes—a popular bike trail.*

ACCESS: From the Summit Rest Area at the east end of the Government Camp business loop, drive 1.5 miles **west** on Hwy 26 and turn *right* (north) onto Rd #522 between mileposts 52 and 53—almost opposite the west entrance to Ski Bowl. There is ample parking (Glacier View Sno-Park) ~200 yards from the highway, and a porta-potty.

Little Zigzag River

MIRROR LAKE AND TOM DICK & HARRY VIEWPOINT

The most popular trail on Mt Hood to a lake that—as its name suggests—mirrors Mt Hood and offers swimming, fishing and a few campsites. Its popularity means that it's hard to escape from the crowds. The hike to the viewpoint is worth the climb and leaves most of the crowd behind.

DIFFICULTY: Easy to Mirror Lake, 700 feet elevation gain; **Moderately Strenuous** to Viewpoint, 1400 feet elevation gain

DISTANCE: 3.2 miles round-trip to Mirror Lake, 2-2½ hours; 6.4 miles round-trip to viewpoint, 4-5 hours. Trail around the lake ~0.5 mile

MAPS: Trail #664 Mt Hood Area Hiking, Riding & Climbing Map, Adventure Maps; National Geographic #321 (Mount Hood Wilderness)

DESCRIPTION: The Mirror Lake Trail is understandably popular as it offers a very gradual trail leading to a well-placed, pretty lake that (when it's still) truly mirrors Mt Hood. The trail climbs 1.6 miles in gentle loops then zigzags and forks just before it reaches the lake. Both forks lead to the 0.5 mile trail that loops around the lake. The *right* fork also leads to the trail up to Tom Dick & Harry Mountain. This trail leaves the main trail just after it reaches the lake and climbs gradually but steadily to a rocky viewpoint on one of the three summits of Tom Dick & Harry Mountain. The additional 1.6 miles to the viewpoint on Tom Dick & Harry Mountain are well worth the effort as there is a spectacular 360-degree view of Mt Hood, Mt Rainier, Mt Adams, Mt St Helens and the Salmon-Huckleberry Wilderness. There are also more flowers on this section of the trail, and huckleberries in the fall. The well-marked trail passes a large cairn of rocks and ends at the first summit.

Spectacular views of Mt Hood reflected in Mirror Lake, a scenic and comfortable picnic site, a swimming beach and campsites all add to the attractiveness of this lovely hike. The trail to the lake passes through a magnificent grove of Douglas-fir trees and opens onto a rockslide where you can hear the bleating of the little rock rabbits (pikas). There are banks of rhododendrons in early summer, and a sprinkling of other flowers later. Small beaches make swimming enticing in hot weather. The lake is stocked although the fish are small. There are campsites at the southwest end of the lake. Usually the area has lots of children, dogs, and large groups, and it is showing signs of use.

Mirror Lake

ACCESS: The trailhead (currently, early 2017) is on the **south** side of Hwy 26 between mileposts 51 and 52, 2.2 miles **west** of the Summit Rest Area (porta-potty) but will be moved in 2018 (along with most of the trail) to start at a new parking area closer to Ski Bowl West Ski Area.

OPTIONAL ADD ON: It is possible to continue after the Tom Dick & Harry Viewpoint on a very faint trail, below the rocky top of the ridge, that will take you over to the top of Ski Bowl (see the *Adventure Map*), from which take the Skyline Rd down to the Ski Lodge. Only for the adventurous—the mountain trail bikes have right-of-way!

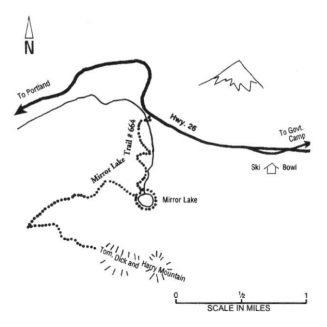

West Fork Falls

This hike offers a hidden and virtually unknown
falls, a delightful mountain stream, huckleberries in
August and mushrooms in the fall.

DIFFICULTY: Moderately Strenuous to falls, 800 feet
elevation gain

DISTANCE: 3 miles to falls, 6 miles round- trip, 3½
hours plus depending on how you return to the Summit
Rest Area

MAPS: This hike isn't shown on any of the area maps but
the Tie Trail linking West Leg Road to the Timberline
Road (#663B) is shown in both National Geographic
Maps: Mount Hood, Mt Hood & Willamette National
Forests, National Geographic #820, #321

DESCRIPTION: This hike is virtually unknown and
seldom used but can be a perfect half-day hike or a
leisurely day hike, especially on a hot day, with opportunities to linger along the way. Uphill grades are mostly
gentle. Most of the hike is on forest roads or trails. The
West Fork Falls Trail is not signed or maintained by the
Forest Service, so follow the instructions or the map below.

From the Summit Rest Area, follow the service road up
the left side of the ski area, behind the Day Lodge, to the
top of the chairlift. Continue on the forest road passing
to the left of the lift. This is the end of Alpine Ski Trail
from Timberline Lodge. Continue up Alpine Trail for
~0.3 mile until you can see a paved road—West Leg
Road—on the *right*, close to the trail. Bear *left* up West
Leg Road for ~0.5 mile to a *left-hand* bend where an

unpaved road takes off to the *right*, signed as East Leg Trail to Snowbunny Lodge. Continue down East Leg Trail, looping over Still Creek (looking at the waterfalls on either side) and down a gentle grade for 0.7 mile. The trail junction is on the *left*, but has no marker (may be a small cairn of rocks) so watch your distance. If you reach the Timberline Road, backtrack for ~0.15 mile. The falls are ~0.6 mile; there will be blowdowns on the trail.

OPTIONAL ADD-ON. This adds additional distance and brings you back down the West Leg Road or up West Leg Road to the Timberline Ski Area and to Timberline Lodge. The witch's warning is that you should only consider this extension of the trail if you are ready to do some bushwhacking. To do the loop, continue on past the falls, crossing the stream and follow the trail on the *right* bank passing three sets of falls that join the stream on the *left*. The trail then follows and crosses a dry streambed. Here the trail peters out but you can continue up the dry streambed and look for a faint trail that climbs the bank on the *left* and leads up to a deactivated service road. Or alternatively just bushwhack up the steep bank on the *left*, and scout around in the open (and lovely) forest looking

for a service road (probably on your *right*) that will take you back uphill to West Leg Road. (If you fail to connect with the service road, retrace your path to the falls).

Once on West Leg Road, either turn *left* to return to the Summit Rest Area or turn *right* to continue up to Timberline Lodge (and reward yourself with drinks

Beargrass

and a meal) or return to the Summit Rest Area via the Alpine Trail. If you decide to turn *right*, continue up West Leg Road on for ~1 mile, passing the bottom end of the Pucci Chairlift on your *right* and under the Flood Chairlift until you see the Stormin' Norman Chairlift just below the road on the *left*. The very rutted, signed Alpine Trail starts just below, and to the *right* of Stormin' Norman, and will lead you down to the Summit Ski Area and the Rest Area. Alpine Trail is a huckleberry heaven in August, and often a silent army of beargrass in a good year.

ACCESS: Park at the Summit Rest Area at the **east** end of the Government Camp business loop.

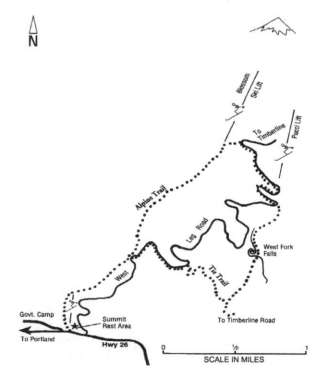

MULTORPOR MOUNTAIN VIEWPOINT

A steep but short climb on an unmarked and un-maintained trail to the top of Multorpor Mountain. Fantastic views in every direction.

DIFFICULTY: Moderately Strenuous; short but steep ascent & descent, 750 feet

DISTANCE: 2.5 miles round-trip, 1- 1½ hours

MAPS: Mt Hood Area Hiking, Riding & Climbing Map, Adventure Maps Inc.

DESCRIPTION: This short, steep hike on an unmarked and un-maintained trail to the top of Multorpor Mountain offers a spectacular, bird's eye view of the area: north to Government Camp and Mt Hood, south to Summit Meadows, Trillium Lake, and Still Creek, and west to Tom Dick & Harry Mountain and Zigzag Valley. The flute-like song of the hermit thrush provides a musical accompaniment. Bunchberries, several different penstemon, paintbrush, cat's ear lily, vanilla leaf, beargrass, anemone, lupine, pyrola and clintonia can be seen beside the trail. Watch your step on the steep ascent and uneven descent. Hiking poles recommended.

ACCESS: Park at the Summit Rest Area at the **east** end of the Government Camp business loop, cross Hwy 26 (carefully) and follow the service

Cat's Ear Lily

road at a brown sign for Timberline Lodge. Pass the power substation and walk on for 0.25 mile to a service road on the *left*, beside a power line. Follow this up a short hill and just after the crest of the hill, as the road is going downhill, ~175 yards from the intersection, find an unmarked, but clearly visible trail on the *right* heading straight up Multorpor Mountain. The trail climbs steadily and quite steeply to the viewpoint at the top. Return the same way.

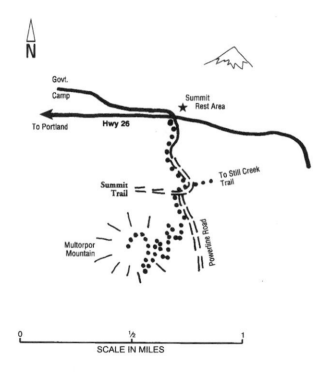

WEST YELLOWJACKET LOOP ❄

This loop is an adventure, since some of it follows a lightly-used cross-country ski trail rather than a well-marked hiking trail, and requires path-finding skills that add to the mystery of this hidden-in-plain-sight hike through beautiful forest and pockets of wetland.

DIFFICULTY: Moderately Strenuous; 700 feet elevation gain, trail indistinct in places—care needed in following the ski trail markers on the trees. A lovely hike for the adventurous. This is a perfect XC/Snowshoe trail in good snow conditions.

DISTANCE: 5 mile loop, 3½-4 hours

MAPS: Cross-country trail **#674**. The best maps for this hike are the National Geographic Maps #820, #321 Mount Hood (Mt Hood & Willamette National Forests, Mt Hood Wilderness); Mt Hood Winter Trails Map

DESCRIPTION: The first requisite for this interesting hike is a sense of adventure as you aren't following a well-marked trail. This is a cross-country ski trail in winter (#674) so, for much of the trail, the path is not obvious. The adventure comes in the challenge of following the trail by looking for the blue diamond-shaped cross-country ski trail markers high on the trees (many of which are attached to blowdowns or may be found on the ground). The key is to make sure that you can see the next ski trail marker before you lose your last one. This hike works better if you have more than one person searching for the elusive ski markers so that one person can stand by the last marker while others hunt for the next one. This hike provides a lot of variety as

it includes easy forest roads, open and new-growth forest juxtaposed with some majestic old-growth trees, moss-covered stumps, a mini-wetland with log bridges over sparkling streams, and plenty of animal tracks.

The marshy areas have many flowers, especially the lovely monkey flowers that thrive in the wetlands and by the streams.

Monkey flower

From the Summit Rest Area, follow the service road up the *left* side, behind the Day Lodge, to the top of the chairlift. Continue on the forest road to the *left* of the lift. This is the end of Alpine Ski Trail from Timberline Lodge. Continue up Alpine Trail for ~0.3 mile until you can see a paved road—West Leg Rd—on the *right*. Turn *left* up West Leg Rd for ~0.5 mile to a *left-hand* bend where an unpaved road takes off to the *right*, signed as East Leg Trail to Snowbunny Lodge. Continue down East Leg Trail, looping over Still Creek (look at the waterfalls on either side) and down a gentle grade for ~ 0.75 mile to meet the Timberline Rd. After crossing the Timberline Rd (carefully), continue on the forest road towards Snowbunny Lodge for ~0.5 mile to a fork. Take the *right* fork for 25 yards and look high up on the bank and see a sign for Yellowjacket Ski Trail and White-a-Way Trail. Climb the bank and look for blue diamond-shaped cross-country ski trail markers on the trees. *Follow the markers, always keeping the next one in sight.* Where the trail meets a forest road, the *left* fork is signed White-a-Way Trail. Take the *right* fork and follow the road for 100 yards, watching for the blue markers. The signed continuation of Yellowjacket Trail is on the *left* of the road, then twists and turns and continues gently downhill through the forest and several areas of wetland (with some huge blowdowns) and comes out just above the junction of Timberline Road and Hwy 26. Watch for a black arrow in the blue ski trail markers in a few places where the trail takes a turn. There will be some very large blowdowns towards the end of the hike. *Always look for the next blue diamond cross-country trail marker before losing sight of the last one!*

ACCESS: Park at the Summit Rest Area at the east end of the Government Camp business loop.

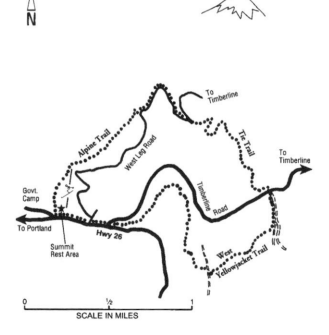

WEST LEG ROAD – ❄
SUMMIT MEADOW – STILL CREEK LOOP

This hike offers great views of Mt Hood, quiet forest roads and a magnificent display of flowers in early summer in Summit Meadow—the site of one of the tollgates on the Barlow Trail.

DIFFICULTY: Moderately Strenuous (easy hiking mostly on roads, 800 feet elevation gain). For an **Easy** walk for those with limited mobility see P82.

DISTANCE: 6 mile loop, 3½-4 hours

MAPS: This hike is a composite of several trails so isn't shown as a specific hike on any of the maps. The most useful maps are the Mt Hood Area Hiking, Riding & Climbing Map, Adventure Maps Inc. and the National Geographic Maps: #820, #321: Mount Hood (Mt Hood & Willamette National Forests & Mt Hood Wilderness)

DESCRIPTION: An appealing hike that loops up from the Summit Ski Area, over to the Snowbunny sledding area, down to beautiful Summit Meadow and up Still Creek Road and a portion of the historic Barlow Wagon Trail. Most of the hike is on forest roads and trails; three 0.5 mile sections are on paved roads with some car or bicycle traffic. Since this loop is a composite of several trails, some attention must be paid to following the directions. It is not far from the beaten track, however, so it is not hard to find your way. A good choice when you would like to walk beside your companions, not in single file. Walking on parts of the Barlow Trail give a great sense of the rich history of the struggles and challenges of the early pioneers who came around Mt Hood rather than brave the dangers of the Columbia on their way to the Willamette Valley. This is a great XC/Snowshoe Loop as a change from the usual tracked trails.

From the Summit Rest Area, follow the service road up the *left* side of Summit Ski Area, behind the Day Lodge, to the top of the chairlift. Continue on the forest road passing on the *left* of the lift. This is the end of Alpine Ski Trail from Timberline Lodge. Continue up Alpine Trail for ~0.3 mile until you can see a paved road—West Leg Road—on the *right*, close to the trail. Bear *left* up West Leg Road for ~0.5 mile to a *left-hand* bend where an unpaved road takes off to the *right*, signed as East Leg Trail to Snowbunny Lodge. Continue down East Leg Trail, looping over Still Creek (look at the waterfalls on either side) and down a gentle grade for 0.75 mile until it crosses the Timberline Rd. Continue on the forest road on the other side of the highway for ~1.5 miles until it reaches Hwy 26, just after the Snowbunny sledding area.

Cross Hwy 26 (very carefully) and walk 0.5 mile down Rd #2656 (may be lots of car traffic) towards Trillium Lake for 0.4 mile to the bottom of the first hill. Where the road flattens out, there is an intersection on the *right*, signed Summit Meadow. Take this and follow the road round to the large open meadow, Summit Meadow. The road skirts the main meadow, passes the Pioneer Baby's Grave on the *left* by the private cabins, and comes to a junction. Just before the junction, opposite the Pioneer Baby's Grave (1882), there is an information board (Tele Tales) that gives a phone number (503-342-3597, 21#) to hear the history of Summit Meadow in the late 1880s.

At the junction, the *left* fork curls back to Trillium Lake (E Chimney Rock Rd). Continue *straight* on E Perry Vickers Rd passing Still Creek Campground on your *right* and continuing straight (don't take the *right* arm of the campground loop) until you see an unsigned trail junction on the *left* beside a notice board. Immediately cross Still Creek on the bridge. This is the Still Creek Trail, part of the historic Barlow Wagon Trail. Turn *left* up the trail (ignoring a side trail to the *left* after ~0.3 mile) and follow it until it reaches the Forest Service cabins on Hwy 26, just opposite the Summit Rest Area.

ACCESS: Park at the Summit Rest Area at the **east** end of the Government Camp business loop.

EASY OPTION FOR THOSE WITH LIMITED MOBILITY: Drive down to Summit Meadow, check out Pioneer Baby's Grave, listen to the Tele-Tales & imagine you are back on the Barlow Trail in your wagon in the late 1880s.

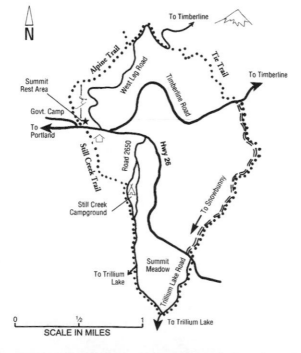

LONG HIKES

RAMONA FALLS LOOP

A classic Mt Hood hike that combines all you want in a day hike in the Mt Hood Wilderness: dramatic views of the mountain, a gorgeous waterfall, a wildflower-bordered stream, banks of wild rhododendrons and a crossing of the often unruly and glacial Sandy River.

DIFFICULTY: Moderately Strenuous with 1100 feet elevation gain and a challenging crossing of the Sandy River which is glacial & swift-moving. See P86 for **Easy** option

DISTANCE: 7.5 mile loop with 1100 feet elevation gain, 5-6 hours

MAPS: Trails #797, #2000, #600 Mt Hood Area Hiking, Riding & Climbing Map, Adventure Maps; National Geographic #321 (Mount Hood Wilderness)

DESCRIPTION: The Ramona Falls Loop is often a family favorite as it combines much of what is so special about Mt Hood hikes: an excellent trail that climbs at an easy grade with gorgeous views, wildflowers, a classic waterfall, colorful rocky cliffs and the challenge of a wild river tumbling down, often creating havoc, and always glacial. Making this hike into a loop allows the hiker to see the dramatic examples of how glacier-fed rivers carve their way through the landscape, changing it forever, as opposed to a gentle mountain stream with wildflower-laden banks.

Take the Ramona Falls Trail (#797) from the trailhead for 1.3 miles through open forest with moss-covered rocks that almost beg to be stroked. In some places the trail splits and you can walk up the old road (on the right) or continue on the trail, close to the river. *Sign in at the Wilderness Permit Box.*

Coming up to the Sandy River is quite a shock as the river is a wide rocky scar from the erosion by the many floods that have raged downstream. There is no longer a seasonal bridge over the Sandy River, but the place where you cross the river is obvious and usually has a fallen tree strategically placed to help with the crossing. Take care, as the river is turbulent and glacially cold.

Once over the river, follow the trail outlined by rocks, cairns or logs to find the trail at the far side, signed to Ramona Falls #797, and a fork ~0.3 mile after the bridge. The loop starts at the fork: you can go *left* up the north arm of the loop or *straight ahead* up the south arm. Parts of both arms are on a section of the Pacific Crest Trail #2000 and a short section is on the Timberline Trail #600. The *left* (**north**) arm is more lush and scenic. The *right* (**south**) arm leads upward toward views of Mt Hood at a gentle grade through open forest with luxuriant banks of rhododendrons; the trail parallels the Sandy River, which is always within earshot on the right. 1.6 miles from the river crossing, the trail meets the Timberline Trail #600. Take the *left* fork and continue 0.5 mile to Ramona Falls—a perfect place for a picnic or just gazing mesmerized by the falls. To return on the north side of the loop, follow the trail past the falls and at a fork, take the *left* arm through beautiful

Ramona Falls

forest and beside a beautiful, tranquil stream bordered by imposing rock formations. My preference is to go up the *right* arm and down the *left* arm but either way works well.

EASY OPTION FOR THOSE WITH LIMITED MOBILITY: The almost-flat walk from the trailhead to the Sandy River crossing is 1.3 miles through beautiful open forest with moss-covered rocks.

ACCESS: From Portland take I-84 **east** to Exit 16, signed to Gresham & Mt Hood & after 2.5 miles, turn *left* (**east**) onto Hwy 26 (Burnside) for 25 miles & turn *left* (**north**) onto Lolo Pass Road (#18). Continue on Rd #18 for 4.3 miles. Turn *right* onto paved Rd #1825, drive 0.7 mile turn *right* across a bridge and drive 1.7 miles to a junction. At the junction, take the *left* fork onto Rd #1825-100, signed to Ramona Falls Trail #797, to a large parking area with a porta-potty.

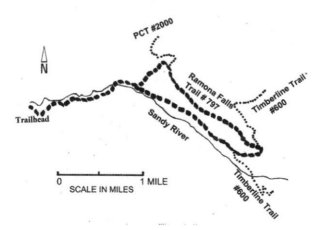

PARADISE PARK LOOP

This is the classic Mt Hood hike in July and August
when the wildflowers carpet the mountain side, views
of Mt Hood still have a snow cover, and the streams
keep everything lush.

DIFFICULTY: Very Strenuous because of the distance, elevation gain of 2300 feet, and hiking at 4000 feet altitude

DISTANCE: 12.4 miles round-trip, 7-9 hours

MAPS: Trails #600, #2000, #757 Mt Hood Area Hiking, Riding & Climbing Map, Adventure Maps; National Geographic #321 (Mount Hood Wilderness)

SHORTER OPTION: Hiking to Paradise Park and foregoing the Paradise Park Loop will cut 4.5 miles off the total distance but will not reduce the elevation gain significantly.

DESCRIPTION: The Timberline Trail #600 runs together with the Pacific Crest Trail (PCT) #2000 from Timberline Lodge and is signed as the PCT. This amazing hike takes you along the joint PCT/Timberline Trail for 3.5 miles then heads uphill to loop back over to the main trail after Paradise Park. The whole hike is overshadowed by Mt Hood with endless vistas to the south featuring Mt Jefferson, the Three Sisters, Olallie Butte, Trillium Lake, and the Salmon Huckleberry Wilderness. For the wildflower lover, this hike is almost unbeatable as the mountain side is ablaze with wildflowers from mid-July through August, especially near the streams. Your progress may be slowed down by the compulsion to identify or photograph the flowers and views! The destination, Paradise Park, has the most impressive display of wildflowers perched below the mountain's glaciers and summit.

Hikers have two options for picking up the Timberline Trail from Timberline Lodge: either start on the Mountaineer Trail or directly on the combined Timberline Trail/ PCT. To start on the Mountaineer Trail, turn *right* coming out of the main Lodge doors and follow the paved road that passes above the bottom of the Magic Mile Chairlift. Where the road forks, just past the lift, take the *left* fork (Mountaineer Trail) and immediately look for a sign for the PCT at the far end of a small parking area for service vehicles. The Mountaineer Trail and the Timberline Trail/PCT join after 0.6 mile. To start on the combined Timberline Trail/PCT, turn *left* coming out of the main Lodge doors, find a paved service road and follow it up a short distance to where the Timberline Trail/PCT cross the service road and turn *left* onto this trail. You are now on the combined Timberline Trail and Pacific Crest Trail. *Be sure to sign in at the Wilderness Permit Box.* Continue on the joint Timberline Trail/PCT heading west, passing the trail to Hidden Lake #779 1.4 miles from the Lodge and dipping in and out of two shallow canyons, Sandy and Little Zigzag. The trail then

drops 750 feet into Zigzag Canyon, and crosses the head-waters of the Zigzag River (here only a stream) ~3.6 miles from Timberline Lodge. This is an easy crossing!

As you pull out of the canyon, just before you reach the top, the trail divides: the right fork, the Paradise Park Loop

#757, climbs 720 feet to Paradise Park—a beautiful alpine meadow—and rejoins the main Timberline Trail/PCT in 2.5 miles. Turn left onto the Timberline Trail/PCT and return to Timberline Lodge. Keep some of your energy for the very long haul out of Zigzag Canyon towards the end of the hike.

ACCESS: From Portland take I-84 east to Exit 16, signed to Gresham & Mt Hood. Follow signs to Mt Hood and after 2.5 miles, turn *left* onto Hwy 26 (Burnside) and drive for 42 miles to the Summit Rest Area at the far (**east**) end of the Government Camp Loop. The road to Timberline Lodge is just past the Summit Rest Area on the *left* (**north**) side of the road. The parking lots for the Lodge are 5 miles up the Timberline Road.

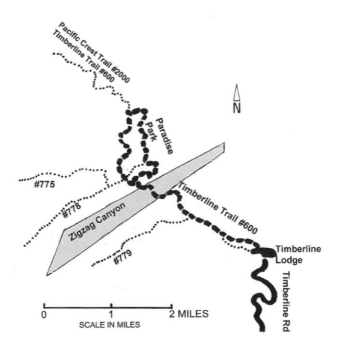

ELK MEADOWS TRAILHEAD– UMBRELLA FALLS LOOP VIA THE TIMBERLINE TRAIL

This hike is hard to beat but, at almost 8 miles, it isn't a walk in the park. The views in every direction are spectacular. Many small streams cross the trail, each one lined with glorious masses of riotous flowers. A short side trip to Umbrella Falls is an added bonus.

DIFFICULTY: Strenuous 2049 feet elevation gain and crossing of Clark Creek. **Moderately Strenuous** 978 feet elevation gain if hiked one-way from Umbrella Falls Trailhead to Elk Meadows Trailhead

DISTANCE: 9.3 or 8.8 miles with two options for last segment of the loop; 7.2 miles for one-way option. 5-7 hours depending on direction & distance

MAPS: Trails #645, #667, #646, #600 Mt Hood Area Hiking, Riding & Climbing Map, Adventure Maps; National Geographic #321 (Mount Hood Wilderness)

OPTIONS: This hike can be shortened to 7.2 miles (with less elevation gain) by using a car shuttle with one car at the Umbrella Falls Trailhead and the other at the Elk Meadows Trailhead. Two options are described for the last segment of the loop.

RIVER CROSSING: There is one river crossing on the Timberline Trail section, Clark Creek. Somehow the word creek doesn't seem appropriate for this, often turbulent, body of water which has multiple channels. As always with river crossings on the Timberline Trail, remember that the water is glacial and take time to scope out the best site to cross. See the section on River Crossing on page 7.

DESCRIPTION: This hike traverses the Mt Hood Meadows Ski Area on a section of the Timberline Trail (#600) using the Elk Meadows and Newton Creek Trails (#645/646) to access the Timberline Trail. The Timberline Trail section is on meadows that are ski runs in winter so there isn't much shade on a hot summer day. There is one river crossing. The main riotous display of wildflowers is on the Timberline Trail segment of the hike with some on the Umbrella Falls Trail but very few on the Newton Creek Trail.

The loop starts at the Elk Meadows Trailhead with an information board and signage to Elk Meadows Trail (#645) and Umbrella Falls Trail (#667). Follow the trail for 1.1 miles, passing the Umbrella Falls Trail #667 on the *left*, and crossing Clark Creek on a sturdy bridge. The junction of the Newton Creek Trail #646 is just over 0.5 mile after Clark Creek on the *left*, before you see the raw gash of Newton Creek. Take the Newton Creek Trail and climb gently for 2 miles through shady forest, parallel to Newton Creek with impressive views down into the canyon carved by the river. The last section of the trail, before it reaches the Timberline Trail, climbs steeply in two long zigzags. At the T-junction with the Timberline Trail #600, take the *left* fork.

After ~1.3 miles on the Timberline Trail, the trail descends to, and crosses, several channels of Clark Creek then climbs again passing through some lightly forested areas, crossing small streams, and passing through the lush open meadows of the winter ski runs for Mt Hood Meadows Ski Area. Several service roads for the ski area cross the Timberline Trail but ignore these and continue traversing the slopes. There is minimal elevation gain or loss and the hiking is easy and very beautiful. Be prepared for frequent stops to admire the views, identify flowers or take photos. The wildflower-lined stream banks are particularly spectacular.

The well-marked trail junction to the Umbrella Falls Trailhead that marks the end of the Timberline Trail segment comes just after a main Mt Hood Meadows service road crosses the trail. At the junction take the *left* fork, signed to Umbrella Falls #667, which leads downhill another 1 mile, over a pretty stream and through beautiful forest and lush lupine-filled meadows to the trailhead on the Mt Hood Meadows Ski Area access road.

To complete the loop, cross the road and pick up the next segment of the Umbrella Falls Trail. The lovely Umbrella Falls is 0.25 mile from the road. Continue on the Umbrella Falls Trail to a fork. For the slightly shorter return to the parking area, *continue straight*, now on the Sahalie Falls Trail #667C, or for the slightly longer option, take the *left* fork, the continuation of the Umbrella Falls Trail.

The Sahalie Falls Trail descends through the forest at a gentle grade for 1.6 miles and merges onto a paved road that leads (*right*) to a viewpoint for the Sahalie Falls. Towards the end of the trail, there is an option to take a somewhat precipitous trail to view the falls. Once on the paved road, either take the continuation of the trail directly across the road to return to the Elk Meadows Trailhead parking or follow the road *left* to the parking area.

The Umbrella Falls Trail loops up to the *left* from the fork, crossing more of the ski runs (more gorgeous wildflower-bordered streams) then heads down to meet the Elk Meadows Trail (#645). Turn *right* for the 0.4 mile to the parking area.

ACCESS: If you want to use a car shuttle, leave one car at the Umbrella Falls Trailhead and the other at the Elk Meadows Trailhead.

Elk Meadows Trailhead: From Portland take I-84 **east** to Exit 16, signed to Gresham & Mt Hood. Follow signs to Mt Hood and after 2.5 miles, turn *left* onto Hwy 26 (Burnside). Drive 41.2 miles to the junction with Hwy 35. Take Hwy 35 signed to Hood River for 7.9 miles to the Elk Meadows Trailhead signed to the *left*. The trailhead is < 0.25 mile on the *right* and has ample parking and a porta-potty.

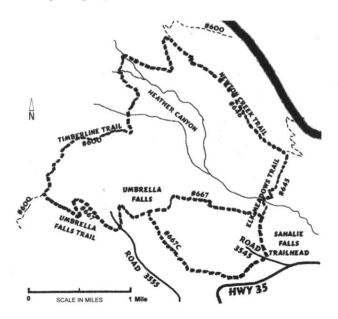

Umbrella Falls Trailhead: From the junction of Hwys 26 & 35, drive north on Hwy 35 for 6.8 miles to the exit for Mt Hood Meadows Ski Area access road. You will exit on the *right* but cross over the highway. The Umbrella Falls trailheads are another 1.5 miles on either side of the road, 0.2 mile before the main Mt Hood Meadows Ski Area parking lot. Look for the trailhead signs above the road in the trees on *left* and below the road on the *right* and park on the shoulder.

ELK MEADOWS

A very popular hike near Mt Hood Meadows that is an interesting mixture of open forest, an exciting crossing of Newton Creek, an uphill zigzag slog and a huge meadow with wildflowers, imposing views of Mt Hood and private campsites.

DIFFICULTY: Moderately Strenuous, 1232 feet elevation gain

DISTANCE: 4.6 miles round-trip to the perimeter trail, 1.5 miles around the perimeter trail. Total 6.1 miles including perimeter trail. 3-5 hours depending on how long you linger and look at the views

MAPS: Trails #645. #645A. Mt Hood Area Hiking, Riding & Climbing Map, Adventure Maps; National Geographic #321 (Mount Hood Wilderness)

DESCRIPTION: This hike is justifiably popular as it combines all of the features that make hiking on Mt Hood so rewarding: fantastic views, beautiful open forest, an exciting crossing of a glacial stream, wildflowers, huckleberries and opportunities to camp by the meadow. The hike can be lengthened by including other connecting trails.

From the parking area, follow the signs for Elk Meadows Trail #645 for 1.2 miles, ignoring trails to the left (Sahalie Falls Trail #667C, Umbrella Falls Trail #667 and Newton Creek Trail #646) and crossing Clark Creek on a sturdy bridge. *Remember to sign in at the Wilderness Permit Box.*

Crossing the next river is more of a challenge: Newton Creek has gouged a wide riverbed with the river running fast, turbulent and glacial. Take your time to find the best place to cross. This is usually upstream ~50-100 yards where there are often fallen trees that provide a convenient way to cross safely. The next challenge is to find the resumption of the trail on the other side. Other hikers have usually placed a series of small cairns that can lead you to a trail opening which is not obvious.

The trail loops up from the river through a gorgeous forest in eight zigzags, flattens out and comes to a 4-way intersection: Gnarl Ridge Trail #652 to the left and the Elk Meadows Trail straight ahead. Continue on straight and in 0.3 mile come to another intersection: the Elk Meadows Trail continues straight and circles half of the Meadows before heading further north. The trail to the left is the Perimeter Trail #645A that circles the left side of the Meadows and joins up again with the main Elk Meadows Trail forming a 1.5 miles trail around the Meadows (created to keep the hordes off the fragile meadow). Follow the perimeter trail around the meadow in either direction. If you head clockwise, just before you emerge onto the edge of the Meadows, you will pass Trail

Mt Hood from Elk Meadows

#652A on your left that joins up with the Gnarl Ridge Trail #652. Continuing on around the perimeter, you will pass many possible campsites and a shelter with stunning views of Mt Hood. Continue until you meet the trail you came up on. Return the same way.

ACCESS: From Portland take I-84 east to Exit 16, signed to Gresham & Mt Hood. Follow signs to Mt Hood and after 2.5 miles, turn *left* onto Hwy 26 (Burnside). Drive 41.2 miles to the junction with Hwy 35. Take Hwy 35 signed to Hood River for 7.9 miles to the Elk Meadows Trailhead signed to the *left*. The trailhead is < 0.25 mile on the *right* and has ample parking and a porta-potty.

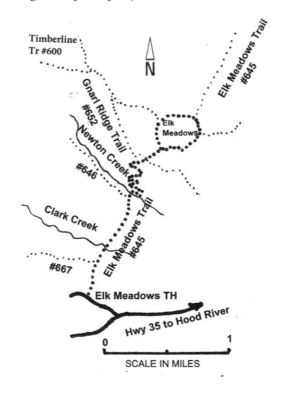

BURNT LAKE

*An exquisite hike through a magical open forest with
wall-to wall carpeting of moss studded with "nurse"
logs growing the next generation of trees. The hike
ends at the lovely Burnt Lake.*

DIFFICULTY: Moderately Strenuous, 1500 feet
elevation gain. For an **Easy** hike, the first 2 miles are
through a magical forest and will work well for those
with limited mobility & kids.

DISTANCE: 6.8 miles round-trip to Burnt Lake, 4- 5 hours

MAPS: Trail #772 Mt Hood Area Hiking, Riding &
Climbing Map, Adventure Maps; National Geographic
#321 (Mount Hood Wilderness)

DESCRIPTION: The first 2 miles of the Burnt Lake Trail
is a magical journey through a mature forest of Douglas-fir,
hemlock and cedar trees that are at all stages of life from
tiny saplings sprouting from "nurse" logs to fallen trees

Trail to Burnt Lake

that are providing the rich mulch for the next generation. Everywhere you look you see an endless wall-to-wall carpet of brilliant green moss studded with an army of "nurse" logs and weirdly shaped roots of fallen trees. The trail climbs very gently for almost 2 miles, then crosses Burnt Lake Creek and climbs more steadily up to the lake. The section up to the creek is the most dramatic by far but continuing up to the lake rewards you with some stunning vistas of Mt Hood, then the jewel, Burnt Lake. The second part, after the stream crossing, has some amazing, huge, old cedar snags that were hollowed out in a fire ~1900.

ACCESS: From Portland take I-84 east to Exit 16, signed to Gresham and Mt. Hood & after 2.8 miles, turn *left* (**east**) onto Hwy 26 (Burnside) for 27 miles then turn *left* (**north**) onto Lolo Pass Road (Road18), just past mile marker 41.5. Continue on Rd 18 for 4.1 miles. Turn *right* onto paved Rd 1825, drive 0.7 mile, turn *right* across a bridge and drive 1.7 miles to a fork. At the junction, take the *right* fork onto Rd 1825-100, signed to Burnt Lake Trailhead and Lost Creek Campground, for 0.3 mile to another fork: the *right* leads to Lost Creek Campground and the *left* fork to the Burnt Lake Trailhead. The trailhead is 1.3 miles further and has a porta-potty.

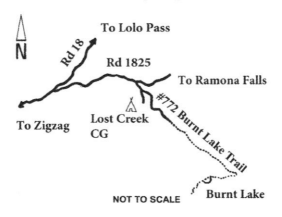

Map of the Timberline Trail

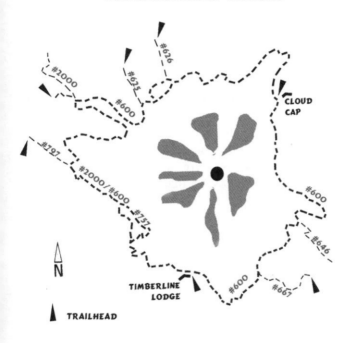

LONG HIKES ACCESSING THE TIMBERLINE TRAIL ON NORTH SIDE OF MT HOOD

VISTA RIDGE TRAIL TO CAIRN BASIN

This hike takes you up to the Timberline Trail from a trailhead on the north side of Mt Hood. It gives you access to Eden Park and Cairn Basin with their extravagant displays of wildflowers in July & August. This is an amazing hike with flower-bordered creeks, magnificent views of Mt Hood with folded glaciers and precipitous slopes. The Vista Ridge Trail and parts of the Timberline Trail on this segment were heavily damaged by the Dollar Lake Fire in 2011 and provide the hiker with the rare opportunity to see the forest's process of recovery.

DIFFICULTY: Strenuous (there & back to the Timberline Trail) or **Very Strenuous for the loop:** 1400 feet elevation gain for the whole loop and 1 or 2 sporting crossings of Ladd Creek

DISTANCE: 5 miles round-trip to the Timberline Trail; 8.5 miles for the loop through Eden Park and Cairn Basin, 4 hours round-trip to the Timberline Trail; 5½ -6½ hours for the loop

MAPS: Trails #626, #600. #600H Mt Hood Area Hiking, Riding & Climbing Map, Adventure Maps; National Geographic #321 (Mount Hood Wilderness)

Avalanche Lilies

DESCRIPTION: The Vista Ridge Trail is a fantastic hike on one of the access trails to the Timberline Trail on the north side of Mt Hood. Its only drawback is the long drive to the trailhead but the rewards are arguably the most extravagant display of wildflowers during July and August both on the Vista Ridge Trail and, once you are on the Timberline Trail, in the exquisite Eden Park and Cairn Basin. The hike can be a round-trip hike up to the Timberline Trail, or extended by hiking clockwise or counterclockwise on the Timberline Trail to make it into a loop. This adds the challenge of crossing the often turbulent and glacial Ladd Creek twice; so take this into account when making a decision as to how much to tackle. See Introduction page 7 with hints about river crossings.

The trail starts at the end of the parking lot and heads upward at a very gentle grade through young hemlock and into cool shady mature forest with moss-festooned trees. There is a rich undergrowth of huckleberries, beargrass, rhododendrons and moss-covered rocks. At a T-junction in 0.25 mile, take the *right* fork (left fork goes to Red Hill Road), signed to the Timberline Trail 2.5 miles. *Be sure to sign in at the Wilderness Permit Box.*

The trail heads up Vista Ridge initially through open forest but almost immediately enters the Dollar Lake Fire burn area on Vista Ridge and passes in and out of the burn area all of the way up to the Timberline Trail. The burned forest has its own beauty with weirdly shaped peeling trees and blackened stumps that may take years to be integrated into the forest floor, mixed in with fresh new undergrowth pushing through the scorched earth. The avalanche lilies are coming back with vigor and almost endless vistas of these beautiful windmill-like flowers carpet the forest floor. Other flowers to look for include beargrass, Indian Paintbrush, shooting stars and Partridgefoot. The grade is mostly gentle and easy walking. To the *left*, there are views of Mt Hood Village on Hwy 35; Mt Adams and the eastern plateau of the Columbia Gorge can be seen in the distance. Mt Hood is in sight most of the time because the Dollar Lake Fire burned most of the trees on Vista Ridge in 2011. The trail joins #600H (an unsigned, alternative section of the Timberline Trail) at a Y-junction signed to Elk Cove *(left)* and Eden Basin *(right)*.

Mt Hood through burnt forest

There are two options at the junction as this is the start of a possible loop: Both are essentially the same distance and both require a crossing of Ladd Creek. The *counterclockwise* direction may be slightly preferred as it gives a sensational view of exquisite Eden Park with an extravagant display of wildflowers and a lush meadow. This part of the Timberline Trail is called #600H and it rejoins the main Timberline Trail after you climb out of Eden Park. The *clockwise* direction takes you to a junction on the *right* with the main Timberline Trail #600, that climbs to a slightly higher contour and joins #600H in Cairn Basin, just after the stone shelter.

If you opt for a *clockwise* direction, turn *left* at the intersection with the Timberline Trail #600H, and after 0.3 mile look for a trail that takes off to the *right* and climbs up, heading back **west**, drops down and crosses Ladd Creek. This is actually the main Timberline Trail #600 that climbs to a slightly higher contour than the lower arm of the loop (#600H) which it joins in Cairn Basin, just after the stone shelter.

Stone Shelter in Cairn Basin

After the stone shelter, turn *right* onto #600H and descend into the exquisite Eden Park with a riotous display of flowers on both sides of the trail, pass a campground and cross Ladd Creek. Look for a good crossing place, sometimes marked by a cairn. The trail then climbs back to the intersection with the Vista Ridge Trail. Turn *left* onto the Vista Ridge Trail.

If you opt for the *counterclockwise* direction (#600H), turn *right* where the Vista Ridge Trail joins #600H and head down through shady forest (some burned areas) and into a meadow. Lost Lake can be seen to the north. The view of Mt Hood is lost for a while as the trail winds through sections of forest interspersed with meadows. The trail crosses a stream then dips down over Ladd Creek, which may be challenging to cross. Look for a good crossing place, sometimes marked by a cairn. The trail passes a large camping area in Eden Park, makes a wide loop around Eden Park and switchbacks up the hillside (riotous display of wildflowers) into Cairn Basin with spectacular views to the north of Mt Rainier, Mt Baker (on a clear day), and Mt Adams. The trail you are on (#600H) meets the main Timberline Trail (#600) at a T-junction. Turn *left* and loop back to the intersection of Trails #600 and #600H (after a second crossing of the exciting Ladd Creek!). At the intersection of #600 and 600H, turn *left;* the start of the Vista Ridge Trail is 0.3 mile on the *right.* Return down the Vista Ridge Trail to the trailhead.

ACCESS: From Portland take I-84 **east** to Exit 16, signed to Gresham & Mt Hood and after 2.5 miles turn *left* onto Hwy 26 (Burnside). Continue for 25 miles then turn *left* (**north**) in Zigzag onto the Lolo Pass Rd #18 for 10.4 miles to the top of Lolo Pass where Rd #18 takes a *right* turn. Continue on Rd #18, unpaved in some portions, for 10.3 miles and turn sharp *right* onto Rd #16 (paved), signed to Vista Ridge Trailhead, and drive 5.4 miles uphill to a fork. Take the *right* fork, now Rd #1650 for 1.4 miles to a fork. Take the *left* for 2.6 miles to the parking area beside the road.

MAZAMA TRAIL

One of the longest but visually most impressive trails leading up to the Timberline Trail from the north side of Mt Hood. It was badly damaged by the Dollar Lake Fire in 2011. It provides stunning views of Mt Hood and an opportunity to watch the recovery of the forest from the fire (and there are abundant wild-flowers fed by the ash from the fires).

DIFFICULTY: Strenuous, 2288 feet elevation gain, no river crossing

DISTANCE: 6.2 miles round-trip to Timberline Trail; add any additional mileage on the Timberline Trail, 5-7 hrs.

MAPS: Trail #625, #600 Mt Hood Area Hiking, Riding & Climbing Map, Adventure Maps; National Geographic #321 (Mount Hood Wilderness)

DESCRIPTION: The hike up to the Timberline Trail is a very rewarding hike in its own right. The added bonus is that it accesses one of the most spectacular and interesting sections of the Timberline Trail, so don't expect to whiz along without any stops; the scenery is breathtaking and the meadows are ablaze with wildflowers.

Beargrass

The trail starts at the parking lot and almost immediately climbs steeply, initially zigzagging up a talus slope, then continuing to zigzag up to the crest of Cathedral Ridge (the previous name of this hike). The trail continues up along Cathedral Ridge with some steeper grades, interspersed with more gentle stretches. The beargrass and avalanche lilies are luxurious in the open areas. The last stretch before reaching the Timberline Trail is along the side of the ridge with a steep drop-off to the *right*, then beside a rock field on the *left*. Listen for the whistle of the rock-dwelling pikas on the talus slope.

Once on the Timberline Trail, explore to the *right* (**west**) or *left* (**east**) as far as your time and energy will allow. It's all a feast for the eyes.

This trail was badly burned in the Dollar Lake Fire in 2011 and will take years or decades to fully recover. In the meantime, hikers have the opportunity to see the fascinating process of recovery from a bad forest fire, with gaunt burned trees, blackened stumps and branches that have a tragic, fascinating story to tell. The undergrowth below them will work rapidly to recover so that every year will reveal different stages of rejuvenation with new wildflowers, shrubs, and shoots all taking root to rebuild the forest. See page 114 for How the Forest Recovers from Fire.

ACCESS: From Portland take I-84 east to Exit 16, signed to Gresham & Mt Hood and after 2.5 miles, turn *left* onto Hwy 26 (Burnside). Continue for 25 miles then turn *left* (**north**) in Zigzag onto the Lolo Pass Rd #18 for 10.4 miles to the top of Lolo Pass where Rd #18 takes a right turn. Follow Rd #18 southeast for 5.3 miles. Turn right onto Rd #1811 (unpaved and perhaps deeply rutted in places), signed to the Mazama Trailhead, and drive 2.4 miles uphill to the large, open parking area beside the road.

See page106 for Map of Mazama Trail.

Pinnacle Ridge Trail

A seldom-used trail that accesses the north side of Mt Hood and the Timberline Trail. It's fun to try this trail because it is quite different from the other access trails—much less predictable, with some marshy areas, with different flowers and grasses. This trail was badly burned in the Dollar Lake Fire in 2011.

DIFFICULTY: Strenuous, 2200 feet elevation gain

DISTANCE: 6.8 miles round-trip, 5- 6 hours

MAPS: Trails #630, #600 Mt Hood Area Hiking, Riding & Climbing Map, Adventure Maps; National Geographic #321 (Mount Hood Wilderness)

DESCRIPTION: A delightful trail that deserves attention. Its failure to gain attention may be because it is an old trail with some marshy areas and an uneven grade with flat areas and several steep pitches, so it is hard to keep an even pace.

Remember to sign in at the Wilderness Permit Box. The trail starts out more or less flat through open forest of Douglas-fir trees that was badly burned in the Dollar Lake Fire of 2011 but is already recovering rapidly. In the meantime, hikers will have the opportunity to see the fascinating process of recovery from a bad forest fire, with gaunt burned trees and blackened stumps and branches that have a tragic, yet fascinating story to tell. The undergrowth below them will work rapidly to recover so that every year will reveal different stages of rejuvenation with new wildflowers, shrubs, and shoots all taking root to rebuild the forest.

The trail heads to the **west**, deceptively easy and flat initially, but soon begins to climb with short steeper pitches interspersed with flatter sections. The trail skirts around to the *right* of several large outcroppings of rocks and continues to head **west** for a while before turning more directly towards Mt Hood. There are several marshy areas to negotiate and trying to keep your boots dry is futile. Just plunge in and splash over to dry ground. There are also several exquisite meadows, one very marshy, but all with interesting flowers and grasses, and abundant huckleberries. The meadows higher on the trail are much drier and are bordered with heather. Continue up through several dry gullies and across narrow streams to the junction with the Timberline Trail.

Once on the Timberline Trail, explore to the *left* (**east**) to Dollar Lake and Barrett Spur or *right* (**west**) to Wy'East Basin as far as your energy and enthusiasm will take you. It's all a feast for the eyes.

ACCESS: From Portland, take Hwy 26 east to Government Camp and continue **east** for 2.2 miles to the junction with Hwy 35. Take the *right* fork and continue towards Hood River, now on Hwy 35 for 17 miles and turn *left* (**west**) at the sign for the Cooper Spur Ski Area, now on the Cooper Spur Road. Stay on the Cooper Spur Road, passing the Inn at Cooper Spur at 2.4 miles, and continuing on for another 5 miles to a four-way intersection in orchards. Take a *left* on Evans Creek Drive, signed to Laurance Lake. After another 0.5

mile, take a *left* on to Laurance Lake Drive for 4 miles to the dam. Continue past the dam to the Kinnikinnick Campground and a forest road (#2840) on the *left* signed to Elk Cove Trail and Pinnacle Ridge Trail. When the road forks at one mile, *continue straight,* signed to Pinnacle Trail, for 2.4 miles. The trailhead is on the *right,* just before the road ends, and is marked by a noticeboard and Wilderness Permit Box. The forest road from the Laurance Lake campground has a fairly good gravel surface and passenger cars should have no difficulty.

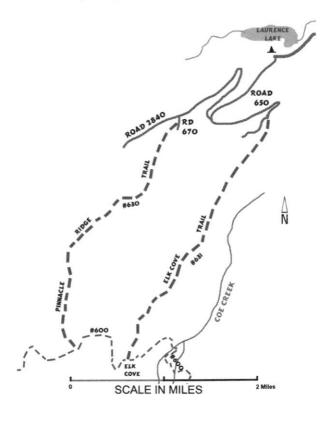

Elk Cove Trail

The Elk Cove Trail is the longest of the trails that access the Timberline Trail on the north side of Mt Hood but the grade is consistently gentle and there are beautiful meadows and views along the way. Even without the added bonus of the Timberline Trail and Elk Cove, this is a sensational hike.

DIFFICULTY: Very Strenuous, 1900 feet elevation gain

DISTANCE: 10.2 miles round-trip plus any additional mileage on the Timberline Trail, 6-8 hours. Maps vary widely in mileage!

MAPS: Trail #631, #600 Mt Hood Area Hiking, Riding & Climbing Map, Adventure Maps; National Geographic #321 (Mount Hood Wilderness)

DESCRIPTION: What more can you ask for? This trail has fabulous views, wildflowers, a good workout, all on a fairly gentle trail, and is usually completely deserted. The trail takes a couple of switchbacks up to a ridge through an area of forest which may be littered with blowdowns as the trail may not be maintained until later in the season. The undergrowth is rich with Oregon Grape, ferns, chinquapin, and kinnikinnick. Look also for twin flowers, lupines and beargrass. Because of the Dollar Lake fire the views of Mt Hood are very dramatic and there are great views down into the canyon carved by the Coe branch of the Hood River. The flowers become more plentiful as the trail climbs. There are whole meadows of avalanche lilies. The trail crosses a beautiful stream about two-thirds of the way up, and the forest and undergrowth become more lush again as they recover from the fire. Marsh marigolds cluster in the wet areas and avalanche lilies carpet the forest floor. The trail then takes a few switchbacks before it opens into Elk Cove. There is a good camping area in the forest just before the trail joins the Timberline Trail.

Once on the Timberline Trail, explore to the *right* (west) or *left* (east) as far as your time and energy will allow. It's all a feast for the eyes.

ACCESS: From Portland, take Hwy 26 east, to Government Camp and continue east for 2.2 miles to the junction with Hwy 35. Take the *right* fork and continue towards Hood River, now on Hwy 35 for 17 miles and turn *left* (west) at the sign for the Cooper Spur Ski Area, now on the Cooper Spur Road. Stay on the Cooper Spur Road, passing the Inn at Cooper Spur at 2.4 miles, and continuing on for another 5 miles to a four-way intersection in orchards. Take a *left* on Evans Creek Drive, signed to Laurance Lake. After another 0.5 mile, take a *left* to Laurance Lake and drive for 4 miles to the dam and lake. Continue past the dam to the Kinnikinnick Campground then take Rd #2840 signed to Elk Cove and Pinnacle Ridge Trails. When the road forks at one mile, take the *left* fork. The last 1.3 miles is rough and narrow in parts, but passable for most passenger cars unless they have very low clearance. The trailhead is on the *left* and marked by a Wilderness Permit Box.

See page 111 for Map of Elk Cove Trail.

How the Forest Recovers from a Fire

*When we see the apparent devastation that results
from an extensive forest fire, we grieve for the loss of
the pristine wilderness, our favorite trails, the flowers,
the animals that live there and other changes in the
ecology of the forest. But fire plays a crucial role in the
life cycle of forests and all of the elements are still there
to allow the forest to be reborn.*

The Dollar Lake Fire on the north side of Mt Hood was
started by lightning in August 2011 and burned more
than 6300 acres before it was put out. Some of the
Timberline Trail and several of the access trails were
extensively burned, but amazingly there are areas in the
path of the fire left essentially untouched. This patch-
work burning is typical of woodland fire and is a result
of the fire burning hotter where there are dead trees or
downed wood that fuel the fire—such as in a forest that

Beargrass with burnt trees

is predominantly Douglas-fir with and dry sunny ridges. Such an extensive fire in a predominantly Douglas-fir forest only occurs every 300-400 years. Amazingly, some of the most beautiful sections of the Timberline Trail, such as Eden Park, Cairn Basin, Elk Cove, Wy'East Basin and Dollar Lake were virtually unscathed.

One of the positive results of the fires that occurred is that the views from the access trails on the north side of Mt Hood and on parts of the Timberline Trail are even more stunning, and we can observe the amazing process of recovery and gain a deeper understanding of how exactly recovery happens. Until the forest recovers, the trails in the burned areas will be blackened and dusty but we will have the rare opportunity to observe firsthand the amazing recovery process, with the dead trees gradually shedding their bark in long peeling strips, revealing a cambium that is often a brilliant chestnut color. If more than 25% of the cambium dies, the Douglas-fir will probably die. If a tree completely dies, the limbs fall off and the tree falls over. This may take up to 20 years.

The sequence of re-growth of the trees is carefully orchestrated. First comes the Lodgepole Pine which needs a forest fire to melt the resin coating on the cones, allowing the cones to open and release the seeds. The seedlings of the Lodgepole Pine can regenerate in two to three years and, as it is a fast growing tree, it provides shade for the young Douglas-fir which is slower to grow and profits from the protection of the taller Lodgepole Pine.

The flowers and undergrowth don't wait for the trees to keel over; they start their recovery immediately. Unlike the trees, many shrubs, flowers and grasses are protected from the lethal temperatures by their soil covering if their roots aren't too shallow. The first to pop up are the wildflowers which appear in even greater abundance right on cue the following spring or summer as the snow melts. The avalanche lilies can put on a spectacular display and carpet the dells with their snowy white windmill tops fluttering in the breeze. The undergrowth and brush start to come up almost immediately as well. This will bring in the wildlife again. The re-birth of the forest is underway.

USEFUL INFORMATION

Mt Hood National Forest:
503-668-1700, *http://www.fs.fed.us/r6/mthood*
Mt Hood Territory Visitors' Center:
888-622-4822, *http://www.mthood.info*
Mt Hood Area Chamber of Commerce:
503-622-3017, *http://www.mthood.org/index.html*
Mt Hood Museum & Information Center:
503-272-3301, *http://www.mthoodmuseum.org*
88900 E Hwy 26 G'ment Camp, OR 97028

Mt Hood's Alpine Village:
http://www.mounthoodinfo.com

Timberline Lodge:
503-272-3311, *http://www.timberlinelodge.com*
Timberline Lodge, OR 97028

FOREST SERVICE OFFICES

Zigzag Ranger Station:
70220 E. Highway 26, Zigzag, OR 97049
503-622-3191

Hood River Ranger Station:
6780 Highway 35, Parkdale, OR 97041
541-352-6002

MOUNT HOOD'S GLACIERS ARE MELTING

The glaciers on Mt Hood feed many of the pristine rivers and streams that provide our drinking water, a habitat for fish, water for agriculture and recreation, and the water used to generate our electricity: an impressive torrent of ~4 billion gallons of water a year. Mt Hood and its glaciers are often used as an iconic image of Oregon. The vision of Mt Hood from Portland has sealed the deal for many who are thinking about moving to Oregon. It's irresistible, even if we can't actually see it every day!

The sad fact is that the glaciers on Mt Hood are melting and retreating. The seven largest glaciers on the mountain have already shrunk an average of 34% since the beginning of the last century, according to Keith Jackson, a graduate of Portland State University, who has been part of a glacier research team funded by the National Science

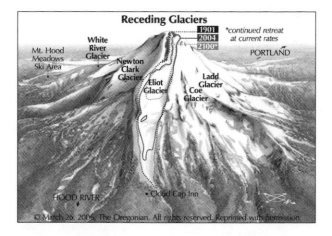

Receding Glaciers

1901
2004
2100*

*continued retreat at current rates

Mt. Hood Meadows Ski Area

White River Glacier

Newton Clark Glacier

Eliot Glacier

Ladd Glacier

Coe Glacier

PORTLAND

HOOD RIVER

Cloud Cap Inn

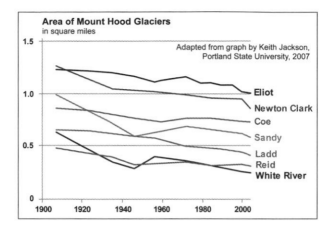

Foundation and NASA. Most climate scientists agree that this dramatic melting of the glaciers is a direct result of global warming.

The consequences of the disappearance of the glaciers are sobering to contemplate. The graphics on these pages tell the story. The warming climate has resulted in torrential runoffs from rapid snow melt combined with rain that have washed out a segment of the Timberline Trail, destroyed bridges, roads and houses, deepened canyons, silted rivers and clogged irrigation systems. When Cloud Cap was an inn, visitors could step out of the door and chip ice for their drinks, or to keep food cool. The glacier toe has now receded for almost 0.5 mile from Cloud Cap. It's hard to guess or extrapolate from the past decades what the future holds for the glaciers on our beloved Mt Hood. We can only hope that they remain and continue to enrich our environment.

Index